Disrupting Divorce

New Rock Press

Seguin, TX

www.newrockpress.com

First Edition

Paperback ISBN: 979-8-9911916-0-9
eBook ISBN: 979-8-9911916-1-6
Kindle ISBN: 979-8-9911916-2-3

Disrupting Divorce:

The New Man

By

Cass Morrow

Contents

Dedication

For my wife, Kathryn, my sweet love, thank you. Without you, I would have never been inspired to rise up into the man I was born to be.

For Castle, Briar, Vale, and Riddick, by the time you grow up, the examples in life all around you will be examples of commitment, follow-through, and true success. Where anything is possible because no one in the world around you will ever remove your choice to be who you truly are.

For men of the world globally, you cannot expect to lead your wife if you cannot even lead yourself.

To my biological and real Dad, Dean Nosworthy, I was fortunate enough to meet you 30 days prior to releasing this book. You are a gentle soul, filled with love as you carry the true spirit of family. What's most remarkable to me, was the instant connection after all the work I have done. Then the instant love, watching you with your grandchildren, I can't help but wonder how different my life would have been had I been raised by you. Both Kathryn and I look forward to making up all the years that were stolen from you and I.

Acknowledgment

To the invaluable authors, coaches, mentors, and influencers:

Your work significantly changed my life. Although I've created my step-by-step system within the Reset, your work was integral to overcoming narcissism, becoming a man and now, a leader in life. From the bottom of my heart, thank you.

Cass,

To my Friends, Brothers, and Lords:

I would also like to express my sincerest gratitude to many Lords from my program. You have all given countless hours to, not only men who needed your support, but to the growth and impact of Morrow Marriage. Your dedication to the vision in my heart, and the world we leave behind, has been insurmountable. I would not be in the position I am in - changing the world – without your energy, your individual experience, and your passion for men to become the leaders in life they were born to be.

You embraced your own growth and continue to lead men, side by side. From the bottom of my heart, Thank you.

In the order you found me and became a Lord:

Andy Doucet
Ryan Brimeyer

Pete O'Reilly
Guillaume Moog
Michael Sherriffs
Greg Hedrick
Matty Sterlo
Dennis Emmitt
Bill Glenn
Rob Richardson
David Waldman
James Tippins

You are all my brothers for life

Cass,

I also want to thank Jelle Dijkstra Photography www.shotsandclicks.com for his wonderful photo for the back cover.

Cass,

Message from the Author

I saved my marriage from the depths of Hell. If you can't save your marriage after I teach you, you don't want to be happy, you're not ready, or you really are an idiot.

Go Get Your Wife.

Cass Morrow

"This book is not for men whose only motive is planned manipulation or control. If you are reading this to hurt your wife with vindictive behavior, contempt-fueled plans, or hold sex as your only motive, this book and its tools are not for you."

Don't Lose Your Wife, Family, and Life. At https://MorrowMarriage.com/Tools, or simply scan the QR code below, you can find numerous resources, tools, and support that will rapidly increase your opportunity for success.

Women, if you're reading this:

This is not to prove you are right, validate you, or supply a tool to beat your husband with. We don't know what we don't know. I would encourage you to be like the many women who have applied my lessons to their lives and saved their marriages. Additionally, if you would like to speak to my wife or learn more about Kathryn's program, The White Picket Fence Project: Keeping Families Together, Kathryn will teach you to stand in your own power and to be the woman you were born to be. Please connect with her on Instagram. Her handle is @kathrynmorrowonline, and her direct link is https://instagram.com/kathrynmorrowonline.

"***Leave it on the nightstand. Listen to our podcast. If he's still not in, you need Kathryn.***"

Foreword

By Kathryn Morrow

I thought he would never change.

"I'm not attracted, not in love, and I'm settling. I'm only here to honor my commitment and my oath under God." Those are the words I said to him when, in my mind, our marriage was over. In fact, it had already been over for years, but until this moment, I was still hanging on, wishing and praying for things to get better. After all, my statement was a subdued version of how I truly felt. There were times I hated my husband; his behavior was not only unattractive, but he had become entirely repulsive, and I teetered between wanting a divorce and completely regretting getting married in the first place.

There was only one thing keeping me from finally leaving—our children. I wanted to keep my family together.

The beautiful byproduct of hanging on for my kid's sake was that my relationship was restored. Expressing my feelings to my husband in a moment of complete despair invoked a beautiful reflection by my husband, and he not only changed the behaviors I desperately needed him to change, but he developed new behaviors that I could never have even dreamed about.

As the author's wife, I want to give you some hope. With the turn of EVERY page of this book, you'll learn tricks, tools, and strategies to save even the worst marriages. I love that my husband has written a book that every man can benefit from—the strategy in this book has no borders. You can use the tricks to break free from toxicity and escape crisis (our specialty) or make your healthy relationship even healthier. As a man, you can finally step into REAL leadership and be the tender and loving man your wife needs while getting your needs met. If you're a woman, try not to cringe as you read that last line—you can read it and then gently slide it onto his bedside table with a bookmark in your favorite chapter, and I'd encourage you to reach out to me to start your journey as well.

I am now a Gottman-trained marriage coach, founder of The White Picket Fence Project, and international best-selling author. I coach women in relationships just like mine used to be—women who are at the end of their rope but believe there must be more, women who probably should leave…but don't.

We are disrupting divorce.

A successful marriage means falling in love over and over again, so if you've fallen out of love, what better time to fall back in love again.

THE RESET

PEACE

MAN IN POWER　　MAN WITH IMPACT　　MAN IN CONTROL

PARTNERSHIP

MAN AT HOME　　MAN WITH KIDS

PASSION

MAN WITH PURPOSE　　MAN AT PLAY

THE 'NEW' MARRIAGE

Introduction

I saved my marriage from the depths of Hell. I'm Cass, a self-aware, managing, severe narcissist, but I didn't know this when I began to rise up and become the man I am today. My past as "Ryan" involved emotional, physical, and sexual abuse towards my wife. My growth began after a court-mandated anger management course as a condition of Kathryn's restraining order, mixed into seven separations, her two divorce lawyers, and my assault charges. One more fuck up, and I was going to jail. Despite these challenges, something shifted during my year of probation.

"If you are not the solution, you are the problem. This is true everywhere in life, especially in your marriage."

You're not as bad as I was—-no doubt—-but just like me, you did not learn to be a man. I was a lazy victim, stemming from the examples my role models in life showed me. I was going to lose it all, and I was a failure. Don't get me wrong, I know how to work. I just didn't know how to me married.

Like I did, you feel inadequate and question your ability to fulfill your roles as a husband, father, and leader. Disrupting Divorce isn't about giving you glorified dating advice or transforming you into an "alpha." It's about real growth. I will make you into the New Man.

"You are responsible for your choices."

This book teaches you how societal norms and male role models have negatively influenced you, led to your failures, and devoured healthy family dynamics. These influences likely robbed you of your ability to find and fulfill your true purpose. But remember that no man is inherently to blame for his situation—we only know what we've been taught; we only know what we know. Further, we don't know what we don't know. Armed with this book and its proven solutions, you now hold the power to make informed choices that will change your life forever.

"You need to mature. Move beyond the "adult boy" you are, and become the man you were born to be."

Be warned! Many men become comfortable and complacent after initially implementing the advice in this book. It's easy to slip back into blaming your wife, quitting, or believing you deserve better.

"It's easy to become a victim."

Your wife should not be your sole motivation when striving to save your marriage, nor should she be your excuse when you're struggling. If that's you, you'll probably not finish this book and quit. You'll continue your old ways and try to be the 'fixer.'

"Your way has not worked. Hang in. I got you."

During my year of probation, I reflected deeply and connected my past behaviors to broader ideas of masculinity, victim mentality, and proactive versus reactive responses. An accidental yet genuine reflection occurred with Kathryn that led to a breakthrough realization about what was normal and responsible in our interactions.

I said, "It's amazing! We're fighting every three days." Kathryn looked at me stunned and said, "That's not normal."

This book shares our journey while providing insights and strategies that have helped not just us but thousands of men and women from around the globe. Location, race, culture, length of time married, no matter the "pain, trauma, wounds"...

"Your story doesn't matter. The symptoms, and therefore the treatments, are the same."

If you believe you're alone in your marital struggles, you need to know that you are part of a global pandemic facing the same challenges. Divorce rates are at an all-time high around the world. You may not exhibit the extreme behaviors I once did, but this book is for you if your marriage lacks depth, communication, and true intimacy.

Whether your relationship is nearing its end or simply coasting, the principles outlined here will revive and transform you, your wife, your children, your marriage, and most importantly, your life.

"It's a bold claim, I know. However, to date, 4300 couples in 26 months. 18 countries. Just over 3300 men. I am damn proud."

I will not bullshit you in this book. I don't have time. I am disrupting divorce. This book demands hard work, honesty, and, most of all, a commitment to change.

You'll need to do things that feel uncomfortable and face truths you might prefer to avoid. Your efforts can either forge a renewed, mad passionate marriage or leave things as they are: unchanged. The decision and the work required are entirely up to you.

"I'm not standing outside your house with a ghetto blaster, blasting love songs, reminding you what to do."

Change doesn't happen overnight—you didn't gain 100 lbs. overnight and won't lose 100 lbs. overnight. This book will challenge you to become the leader in your own life while inspiring your wife, children, and the men around you.

"It's a ripple effect happening around you now. Get slammed by the tidal wave or ride it."

You can either perpetuate a cycle of blame and dysfunction, stop the tailspin, and lead a life filled with leadership, passion, and fulfillment.

"Now is the time to learn. If you need more sleep, sleep faster."

If you find a typo or grammatical error in the book, there is a link to a form on my website in the back of the book. Please tell me there instead of leaving a 1-star review.

On the other hand, if you're focused on what this book is about——you'll likely miss these mistakes and leave a 5-star review.

The moment you start to 'click' would be an incredible opportunity to begin leading men worldwide.

A 5-star review can be your first act as the New Man.

Thank you,

Cass

YOU ARE THE BIG BAD RACE CAR.

YOUR WIFE IS JUST THE RACING STRIPES ON THE CAR.

GET HER RIDING SHOTGUN.

GET HER RIDING STICK.

YOU LEAD THE RACE.

What to Expect

Understanding what's required of you is crucial to succeeding with my program, The Reset, and genuinely transforming yourself. Knowledge is power, but understanding my system won't change your dynamic. Instead, we must work together to transform you into the ultimate version of yourself.

"I will build you into a big, bad race car. Your wife is just the racing stripes on your car. I'll get her ridin' 'shotgun'... ridin' stick. But you must be consistent on the track and get in front of the pace car: your wife."

At first, there may be resistance, and she might challenge your changes. She will confront you or even seem to work against you. She's the pace car. The goal is to get her ramming the side of your car, and she might even try to run you off the track or set your wheels on fire! Don't be surprised if she drives right over you. This is all part of the process.

You'll learn to navigate and embrace these challenges and understand that you've allowed her to set the pace for a while, but it's been too long. Although she might be confused by the new you at first, eventually, you'll leave your past in the rearview and move forward together.

"To do this, you must let me pull you out of your comfort zone. You will resist. Don't."

3 TYPES OF WIVES

TYPE 1: THIS IS EVERYTHING SHE EVER WANTED.

TYPE 2: SHE'S IN, SHE'S OUT.

TYPE 3: SHE DOESN'T TRUST YOU.

VICIOUS TYPE 3: CONTEMPTUOUS, MEAN AND ANGRY.

The Three Types of Wives:

"There are three types of wives. Understand them, but don't confine her to one type. She will be a shapeshifter."

Type 1 Wives:

These women love the new man. They will embrace the changes wholeheartedly, exclaiming, "This is everything I ever wanted!" They're quick to adapt and support your new direction.

Type 2 Wives:

These women are uncertain and may flip-flop in their support. One day, they might believe in the changes, and the next, they could doubt their authenticity. This can lead to tension and possible reactive behavior as they process these changes.

Type 3 Wives:

These women are the most skeptical and will actively resist the changes you're implementing. They are upset you didn't make these changes sooner and are filled with contempt or anger. Vicious Type 3's: Sometimes, their resistance can feel like direct sabotage, and she can be reactively abusive.

From personal experience, I learned that persistent effort and consistent behavior are crucial to overcoming skepticism and resistance. My journey involved serious legal and relational challenges with Kathryn, which required me to continually prove my commitment to change, especially when it was "her turn" and she became reactively abusive.

The Reset—my program and unique coaching model—is designed from real-world experiences that include overcoming deep-rooted issues like emotional and physical abuse, narcissism, and other toxic and maladaptive behaviors. By working with thousands of men, I've refined the strategies that lead to lasting change. We'll fine-tune your approach to life while altering your ingrained patterns and the way you think.

"We will replace your bad habits with the right skills."

This journey is about making substantial, second-order changes. These refer to changes that fundamentally alter the dynamics of your marriage. These aren't first-order changes like temporary fixes or even suppressing bad behaviors. We're working for a transformation that makes you a leader and a man your wife wants to follow.

You'll need to replace bad habits and poor skills with solid and constructive skills that build instead of tearing down. This is not about quick fixes but creating a sustainable new you that doesn't appear to be changed but truly has changed.

If you're ready to take this ride, know you're not alone. Join our community of Lords, where you'll find more training, tools, resources, and support from men worldwide facing similar challenges. Together, we'll ensure you have the support you need to succeed.

Check out our podcast Morr Marriage on YouTube, Spotify, and anywhere you listen to Podcast and visit MorrowMarriage.com/Tools for more information and to access the resources necessary for your transformation.

Why Men Fail:

Failure to Implement Fully*:* Men fail most obviously because they don't fully engage with the program. Many don't use it. Watching my training videos, reading this book, listening to my podcast, or browsing social media isn't enough. You can't pick and choose what you want to implement. True transformation requires active engagement—implementation, interaction, reflection, and adaptation—-with all the steps. Real growth happens when you rise up, show up, and continuously strive for improvement. Lords will guide you, but the work is yours alone.

Isolation and the Illusion of Self-Sufficiency:

Many men think they can handle their problems independently. If learning and being alone were enough, you wouldn't need help now. I even use mentors that I have also trained in relationships to help me through difficulties.

"No man is perfect, including me."

This is why our men's group, which we call Lords, is essential. It provides support from like-minded men who are committed to improving themselves and their marriages. More importantly, they also leave a legacy and impact other men worldwide.

"Free mentorship: if you only care about saving your marriage, you will fail."

Misconceptions About Control and Influence:

A significant reason for failure is misunderstanding what and who you can control. You must control yourself! How will you lead her if you cannot make decisions for yourself?

"Don't think for a minute that these areas don't impact every detail of your life and marriage."

I've seen men fail and refuse to apply the conversation strategies from Man with Impact. They choose to defend themselves over learning to have productive and engaging conversations.

In my program, we address this upfront. In a memorable coaching call, I had to call men up, not out, who repeatedly ignored implementing Man at Play. When they ignore these principles, they let their insecurities dominate their actions.

"Might as well call a divorce lawyer now."

I can't count the examples of men who blamed their wives and sat in that pain and resentment. The bottom line? If you can't control and commit to improving yourself—and follow through—you render your wife's follow-through irrelevant.

"Why are you frustrated when your wife doesn't follow you? How can you expect to lead her if you can't first lead yourself?"

Frustration with the Process: Making significant life changes is challenging. When these changes don't immediately resonate with your wife or if she reacts negatively to your efforts, it's easy to become disheartened and, often, defensive.

"You may want to quit."

Remember that these negative patterns didn't appear overnight, and neither will the positive ones. In Man in Power, we focus on reclaiming and embracing your strength by transforming the man you once were into a man who takes responsibility for himself.

It's crucial to understand that setbacks are part of the journey. Success requires persistence and embracing the rigorous work involved. This is going to be hard and can often be slow. Avoid resigning to failure just because the path is challenging. Own your shit, and let me call you up.

"This is why you're in this mess in the first place."

Stay Engaged and Committed: Your wife didn't hope for a life filled with conflict or separation, strife, frustration, or emotional abuse. She doesn't want the kids half the time. She doesn't wish for divorce on her resume, and neither do you.

Focus now and avoid falling into a pattern of excuses or justifying a lack of progress because it's "hard." Being a man worth following means having the strength to handle hard things. If you can't live with yourself through positive transformation, how can your wife live with you as you are?

"The work is hard. Divorce is hard. Choose your hard."

Talking to Your Wife About This Book:

Many of you were introduced to The Reset through your wives, who may already be familiar with my work from social media. Whether she knows or not, this book instructs you about many things. One of them is how to talk with your wife about the path you're on.

For now, be quiet and start learning because when you start talking with your wife about this book and the program, you must approach those conversations much differently than you might think.

Your wife may be curious about what you're learning. She seeks more confidence and assurance in your actions than in your words. Although she may say she wants to know everything going on, deep down, she desires to see the results naturally unfold.

Women appreciate strength and confidence. They want to see that you believe in your actions and embody change rather than just talking about it. Show her, don't tell her!

"Nobody gives a shit about who you're going to be; they only care about who you are, and that's defined by how you've made them feel in the past."

Men Make Decisions Over Their Personal Growth:

You're not expected to ask for permission or approval for every step. This is also true in your marriage and in the bedroom. Constantly seeking approval undermines your wife's confidence in your abilities, making her wonder if you are who you say you are.

This doesn't mean you should hide your journey of personal growth; instead, the specifics of how you're improving should be demonstrated through actions and changes in your behavior.

Answering Your Wife's Questions:

She might question what you're learning or how you're changing, so keep your explanations simple and straightforward. You don't need to dive into every detail immediately—this is something we will explore more deeply in Man in Power and Man with Impact.

Facing Judgment:

It's natural to feel vulnerable when you expose your path to personal growth, especially if you are judged or mocked for your efforts. Remember that the decision to grow and improve is a sign of strength, not weakness.

You may choose to leave this book on your nightstand or openly discuss your participation in courses or men's groups. It is vital to face any skepticism or mockery with confidence. Don't let fears about "sharing too much" with us deter you from your growth.

"Don't ever find comfort in failure with failing people. Lead them."

Embracing this journey publicly highlights your commitment to change and will inspire respect from those around you. You're not merely talking about changes; you're living them. This is how you rise above societal expectations and refuse to settle for mediocrity. Think abou it, I share my story publicly, so I'm forced to follow through. Don't just jump right into this, I will instruct you on how later in this book.

The Role of Sex:

I discuss sex often. It's not because it's the end goal but because it's a vital part of a thriving marriage. Achieving intimacy with your wife means reconnecting on multiple levels, not just physically. It's important to note that a renewed sex life and mad passion are a clear sign that you have reset emotional intimacy in your marriage.

"In marriage, we want to max out your RPMs and redline the shit out of intimacy, but sex is just the checkered flag."

Embrace this path with confidence. Go Get Your Life.

The Peace Pillar

Peace

The first pillar of The Reset is Peace.

Some of you might think, "Cass, I'm not as abusive as you were, so I don't need to bring peace to my home. Our home is pretty peaceful." But peace is about more than the absence of violence or fighting. Many men believe that if they don't physically harm their wives, they don't need to worry about creating and maintaining peace. This misconception misses the more profound point of peace within a relationship.

By stepping into the roles of a Man in Power and a Man with Impact, you'll create an environment where your wife can be herself again, unapologetically. You might think she has already come around, but if neither of you feels fulfilled by the marriage, something is out of place. A home where either spouse walks on eggshells is not peaceful. It's a Cold War zone, even if all seems quiet.

"It's time to sweep up the fucking eggshells."

When you embrace your role as a Man in Power, you will develop your ability to take responsibility, be accountable, and take actual ownership of your life and for yourself. We will harness your inner strength and transform you into the man you were always meant to be. As a Man with Impact, you'll provide the safety needed for your wife to express her deepest feelings and pains, empowering her to lower the walls between you.

"Peace is about safety and trust in your home."

I don't care what emotion your wife needs to feel. My goal is to create a safe space for her to express herself. When she feels secure enough to let her guard down and share her true feelings, she'll knock down the walls that are preventing deeper intimacy. This will bring about fun and flirty conversations, meaningful interactions, and, yes, a fulfilling sexual relationship.

"The needless rejections have to stop."

Imagine living in a home where, no matter what, you choose to stop and laugh through the hard conversations. Isn't that a better way to live? Forget the old mantra that "Communication is key." It's not about communication formalities but learning how to engage in genuine and heartfelt conversation. When you master this, your wife's admiration and respect for you will naturally increase, dissolving any lingering disrespect. She'll revert to her natural, loving, nurturing, and empathetic self. She will be alive again and thrive with you.

Providing this peaceful, supportive environment inspires your wife to follow you and engage actively in the relationship. Kathryn and I not only survived, but we continue to thrive.

"Bring her back to life."

MAN IN POWER

It does not take two.
It takes one to lead

Man in Power

A Man in Power is foundational to setting the stage to become your best and most authentic self. We'll take a deep dive into this in Man in Control. For now, your focus is on taking 100% responsibility for your actions and outcomes in all areas of life—your marriage, business, health, legacy, hobbies, and beyond. It's essential to recognize that your current position in life is the result of your choices—the good and the bad.

Taking Full Ownership: While incredible resources are out there, like Extreme Ownership by Jocko Willink, they often miss something crucial regarding relationships. In my program, taking ownership is about understanding what you want in your relationship with your wife and the personal discipline needed to take full responsibility for the direction of your marriage.

"When you've mastered this in your relationship, the fog lifts, and you will notice more success—even in your most successful areas of life."

Accountability, Not Just Supervision:

Accountability is often misunderstood and oversold. You could hire me to check your diet or prevent you from making defensive remarks to your wife, but true change comes from within. This book is designed to help even the most disciplined man recognize where he needs support by creating internal accountability that transcends external supervision.

"Even the best trainers can't follow you around to slap the food out of your mouth."

"The moment you give up, because you're blaming her, is when she becomes your why not!"

Being a Man in Power is being steadfast in your commitments even when faced with setbacks. It involves staying true to The Reset, reflecting, evaluating, and seeking help when necessary. This is critical when you start spiraling out of control or when your wife becomes your "why not" rather than your "why."

Addressing Masculinity:

Society's idea of masculinity can be confusing. It's often seen as either toxic or counter to modern standards. Lords are redefining masculinity while holding masculine virtues like strength, responsibility, and integrity without surrendering to outdated stereotypes. I will discuss this further in Man with Impact, exploring how embracing your masculine energy can grow your relationship and allow your wife to live freely in her femininity.

Power and Its Application:

Using the systems and tools I've developed ensures that accountability is maintained for a Man in Power. We can't own our outcomes without first accepting responsibility for them. For example, consider the common example of your wife using sex as a weapon. If you reacted defensively to something she said, leading to negative emotions, it's on you to recognize how your actions contributed to the rejection of sex. This isn't just about not being defensive; it's about understanding why you reacted that way and how to change it in the future.

"If you snap at the kids or make a stupid comment, she's not using sex as a weapon; you're the weapon."

Looking for the Green Light:

This is about ensuring all systems are 'go' for healthy, dynamic interactions with your wife. It means moving from defensiveness and miscommunication to a state of open, honest, and constructive conversations that move your entire life forward.

In upcoming lessons about power in Man in Control, I'll dive deeper into how you must maintain your power and avoid falling into the "Nice Guy Triangle." This is where men lose their sense of authenticity in the new man and start blaming external factors for their problems in life. Remember, men take responsibility for everything they are and everything they do. No one else is to blame, ever.

"In the haze, your wife is your easiest target."

Final Thoughts:

Being masculine is about providing structure for the direction of your life. You are responsible for a stable foundation for your relationship where both you and your wife can thrive. As I've already said, the key is to take responsibility for your actions and the emotional safety you create in your home. We will lay the foundation for this by taking responsibility as a Man in Power. Don't worry. You will be given the tools to succeed, but you have to be willing to use them.

This approach is practical and actionable. It's not some set of theories or senseless playtime. By committing to rise up, you will see tangible improvements in all areas of your life. As we step into this power, we'll redefine what it means to be the new man in today's world. This is a good thing and something the world needs right now.

"The New Man is disrupting divorce and making an impact globally."

Your Vows:

Reflecting on your wedding vows is a critical first step toward becoming a Man in Power and embracing full responsibility for your actions. When you stood before your wife, family, friends, and even God (for some of you), you pledged "for better, for worse," and committed to "have and to hold; to love and to cherish," regardless of whether times were "rich or poor," or in "sickness and in health."

"You didn't say unless my wife is disrespectful or doesn't fuck me."

These vows didn't include escape clauses that allowed for scaling back your efforts or withdrawing your affection based on your wife's actions. They didn't provide an out if you decided you had "more important things to do, like work, sports, or friends."

Society might have shifted and is telling us that vows are breakable for any reason—or in the case of no-fault divorce or for no reason at all—leading to skyrocketing divorce rates. This distortion of commitment is why the first thing you need to do is take a hard look at yourself and examine your core values. We'll hash this out when we make you a Man in Control.

"How can you get upset at the unwritten vows your wife has broken if you can't take responsibility for the written and spoken vows you committed to?"

Regardless of how your wife has treated you, you made a promise, "Until death do us part," not "Unless you don't have sex with me." These vows were promises of integrity and honor that men throughout history used to value. Your vows were not conditional contracts. In fact, in many places, you would have been disrespected or shunned for dishonoring your vows in any sense, much more so with a divorce.

Wedding vows are now seen as just another part of the wedding ceremony for many couples and are quickly forgotten after the day has passed. This disregard for vows is precisely why Kathryn and I refer to our podcast, Morrow Marriage, as The "NEW" Marriage.

In this book, you will learn skills to build a new type of marriage—one that breaks free from the mistakes promoted by society, repeated through generations, and even promoted by well-meaning therapists and pastors. It's worth noting that many therapists and pastors join our programs, having seen firsthand the failures of traditional approaches. They come to us seeking a more effective path. They come to us for help.

"At least one man a week tells me his therapist told him to use porn, open his marriage, cheat, lay boundaries, or leave. This is disgusting."

As you're reading this, I want you to focus on aligning your actions with the vows you made. Reflect on what you've done wrong, whether you learned these behaviors directly or indirectly, and recognize where your actions have not upheld the standards of the New Man—the man of which you can and should be (truly) proud. This realization is a crucial part of what you need right now as it will guide your approach to the transformative journey found in this book.

Adult Boys Are Not Masculine:

Simply growing up does not make you a man. Real men own their mistakes and take responsibility for rising up at all costs. When confronted with their past failures, many men default to toxic behaviors like following alpha male stereotypes or using glorified dating advice that exploits negative emotions like insecurity, jealousy, or fear in order to manipulate and regain their wife's affection. These approaches are not only ineffective, but they do great damage and, honestly, destroy the chances of building a sustainable marriage. You will find none of that advice in this book.

Some aspects of your current situation may not be the result of your choices alone. Dr. Robert Glover, in his 2003 book No More Mr. Nice Guy, identified what he calls the Nice Guy Syndrome that affects many men in varying degrees. It's startling how quickly men recognize themselves in the characteristics Dr. Glover describes within the first ten minutes or the first chapter of his audiobook. Dr. Glover's insights are essential to our approach in The Reset and heavily influence our coaching sessions in Lords. We talk a lot about the Nice Guy - and Lords don't like him.

"Understanding how your Nice Guy tendencies impact your reactions to the world will set you free."

You are going to conquer your Nice Guy and all the tendencies that he carries. But you're not just going to be liberated 'from' him; you must be someone else completely to model authentic masculinity to the world around you. The world is desperate for men who rise to this challenge—a challenge you have embraced by engaging with this book.

"The conditions that led you here are insignificant compared to the benefits of doing this work."

I'm often quoted as saying, "Your story doesn't matter. The symptoms are the same; therefore, the treatments are the same." My approach is to replace bad habits with the right skills to create openness and authenticity in your interactions throughout life. Man with Impact will help you release any shame tied to negative influences and connect with the man you will become.

There are two types of Nice Guys: the 'I'm-so-good' and the 'I'm-so-bad' Nice Guy. The former shows affection, then ultimately explodes in anger when he feels that affections are not reciprocated. The latter sabotages himself and undermines the good within him. These behaviors are what Kathryn refers to as dealing with "Nice Assholes," and when a Nice Asshole's needs aren't met, they shift from love to blame.

"At the risk of turning you away now: you are a Nice Asshole."

What kind of man will you choose to be? This isn't about being the toughest or the most accommodating man—no, it's about being true to yourself. Authenticity and confidence cannot be faked, and they must be built through genuine self-reflection and deliberate action. Your wife will know if you are acting. Trust me, she knows.

"Overcome these obstacles. They are holding you back from your marriage's peace, partnership, and passion."

You will be given the tools to maintain integrity and lead a fulfilling relationship. Man in Power, Man with Impact, Man in Control, Man at Home, and Man with Kids will guide you through healing your home and making it a safe and empowered environment. Man in Control and Man with Purpose will help you tap into drives you never knew you had. You will be empowered and energized beyond your own recognition. All this will build in Man at Play when you learn to deepen your connection with your wife and race across the finish line, waving the checkered flag of a vibrant, emotionally connected, purposeful, and intimate marriage.

As you go through The Reset, remember to always focus on maintaining a 'Green Light' in your home. This represents creating an inviting, dynamic, and responsive atmosphere conducive to deep connection and mad passion. Understanding how to achieve this in your home is critical to transforming your marriage and the legacy you build for your family.

Automatic Turn-Offs:

I use this training to bring men into my program from my website. Let me be clear: Automatic Turn-Offs are not about sex. They are about everything men do to turn their wives away, smother them, and make them want space long before sex could ever happen.

All of Society's Solutions are automatic Turn-Offs. Men use them to fix minor issues and big problems and often think they are a precursor to getting laid. These solutions include stupid light bulb moments for men that women have known for years.

"Automatic Turn-Offs are pushing your wife away from conversations to banter. Flirts to dates. And yes, sex."

SOCIAL CUES

ORDER

CHORES

I GIVE

EGO FEEDING

THE "TALK"

YES MAN

SOLUTIONS

Society Solutions:

Automatic Turn-Offs, or "Society Solutions," refers to popular wisdom or strategies used to fix issues and solve relationship problems. These pseudo-solutions are taught as helpful cultural norms and are depicted in television and movies today. Marriage therapists even teach many of them as a way to fix troubled relationships, but in the end, they never address the root cause of marital issues.

D.S.O. does an excellent job critiquing these approaches in his book, The Dead Bedroom Fix, which has influenced most other programs I have seen. While his insights are foundational, my approach diverges slightly from these traditional pseudo-solutions, which, ironically enough, are all spelled out using the word "SOCIETY."

"You won't find this anywhere else; we do things differently."

SOCIETY

S: is for Social Cues
O: is for Order
C: is for Chores
I: is for I Give
E: is for Ego Feeding
T: is for the "Talk"
Y: is for "Yes" Man

Digging deeper into Society Solutions, you'll see their limitations as you remember using them. I was the king of using these 'solutions,' but I failed miserably. I tried all of them without success. The issue arises not from the actions themselves but mainly from the expectation of reciprocation.

Dr. Glover calls these expectations covert contracts, the "give-to-get" mentality. Performing acts of kindness and taking responsibility should stem from your inherent values as a great man, not from a desire for reward or recognition… and especially not romance. I tell you to be an adult.

It's common to see men attempting these solutions only to express frustration when they don't yield the expected return. Statements like, "Hey, Honey, I did X," hoping she'll notice or using these actions as leverage to "prove" your worth. This behavior will eventually set you up for failure. Such approaches not only fail to enhance intimacy but also force your wife to look down on you. And she's not wrong for doing so.

"All respect is lost when your wife looks down on you."

Rather than focusing on how these actions will get you what you want, it's better to focus on the fact that you should want to do these things–anything you do–responsibly because you are an adult. Your efforts should never be transactional. If you're performing actions merely to catch your wife's attention rather than being your most authentic self, she will likely sense your insincerity and react negatively. Think about it. Would you clean, do laundry, or play with the kids because it's what you want to do, or are you doing it out of a desire to be seen doing "good" things?

A note: there are many areas of "doing" that I'll cover later in the book. To simplify the point, anything you do to gain attention so your wife will notice and love you kill the little respect she still holds for you.

As we explore Society Solutions, I encourage you to take responsibility for times you've misused these strategies. Embrace the opportunity to show up as the man you're proud of so that when you look in the mirror, you see a man acting out of integrity and authenticity, not out of a desire for validation.

"If your wife leaves you, you'll have to do all these things without expecting anything in return anyway, so understand them now."

In Man in Power and Man with Impact, we will examine these societal norms and provide alternative strategies that create genuine connection and respect. You will learn to develop a cohesive understanding of how to build a relationship rooted in respect and mutual support instead of a "give-to-get" mentality while focusing on personal growth and genuine interactions. We will transform your relationship and your entire approach to love and life.

Social Cues

"I provide, I protect, I'm a great dad, and I'm a great guy." Let's dissect these claims and what they mean within your relationships as perceived by your wife.

"Ps. I know you've been raised to believe this is what proves you're a great man."

Providing:

You think you're fulfilling your role because you provide financially as you should. Throughout history, men have been "breadwinners," responsible for putting food on the table. The expectation is to earn enough to support the family's lifestyle. You might think, "I'm doing my job, so why isn't that enough?" But simply providing doesn't make you exceptional—it makes you normal.

"If it's normal, you are average."

You've been using this as leverage and asserting to your wife that she should want you because of your financial contributions. But she's probably thinking, "You're supposed to do that, so what else are you bringing to the table?" You continue to build the wall between you.

Security and Safety:

Other forms of security are essential—physical, emotional, and spiritual. You might be a top earner, but if your contributions stop there, you're not addressing her broader needs. It's not about the money and stuff but the emotional connection and security that comes from knowing she can rely on and trust you. Are you just as reliable without cash? If not, you fail to protect her in the most critical ways.

Protection:

The concept of protection makes men think of physical defense, but how often are you sliding across the hood of your BMW to save your wife and family from kidnappers? If you live in a rough neighborhood, you should move. Proper protection involves creating a safe and trustworthy environment. If your wife can't rely on you for tiny promises, how can she trust you in more significant crises? We'll explore this further in Man with Purpose.

"I once had a Lord that said, I sleep through the night. My wife checks out the noises. WTF??"

Parenting:

Being a great dad goes beyond providing, playing with your kids, and disciplining them. It involves emotional engagement, being understanding, and growing alongside them. If you're enforcing rules without understanding their emotional needs, you're not genuinely excelling in your role as a father. We'll dive deeper into effective parenting in Man with Kids, but start examining how you can either reproduce the errors of your upbringing or forge new and healthier patterns for your children today.

Nice Guys Finish Last:

Lastly, being a great guy isn't about fulfilling a checklist of societal expectations. It's about integrity, empathy, and respect in action—not just words. If you're questioning why your efforts aren't appreciated—"I'm such a nice guy, why doesn't she love, respect, or want me?"—it's time to reflect on whether you're genuinely meeting your wife's needs or just ticking your boxes. Real intimacy and respect aren't about doing things to get something in return but about genuine engagement and mutual appreciation.

"The rest of SOCIETY spelled out undermines any greatness you have as the great guy."

Order

Order within relationships goes beyond structure or the lack of chaos. Actual order involves responsibly handling your influence and the power dynamics in the home. Many traditional programs offer solutions that border on manipulation or control, which leads to superficial compliance rather than genuine connection.

Reflect on this: when you issue ultimatums or subtly threaten to seek attention elsewhere—as in the examples of telling your wife, "Fine, I'll watch porn," or "There's a girl at Starbucks I keep ignoring"—you are not creating trust or respect. These are tactics of first-order change, where changes are provoked by fear rather than genuine understanding or desire. These do not last.

You could be super gentle with your words, but you're trying to manipulate her. Saying, "If you don't want me, I could get anybody I want." creates a temporary compliance based on insecurity or fear instead of lasting desire or respect. It's no surprise that any gains in intimacy or positive behavior might quickly evaporate while leaving both of you more distant than before.

Order isn't about asserting control but creating an environment where everyone can grow, and authentic feelings can be expressed. Negative emotions that come from manipulation or control, such as loneliness, emptiness, or isolation, only serve to deepen the tears in your relationship. This effectively sets up a "Red Light" scenario where progress is prevented, and without growth, there's death.

"Grow or die."

We must erase these harmful patterns altogether. This means moving beyond Society Solutions and instead focusing on second-order changes, which involve more profound, systemic shifts in behavior and attitude. These changes are about evolving yourself and your approach to your relationship, not just applying quick fixes.

"If it's not positive, it is negative. You cannot create positive from negative."

The process of creating order involves leading by example and not coercion. It's about learning and implementing strategies that improve your interactions and relationship dynamics. Avoid the rabbit holes filled with deceptive quick fixes that promise immediate results but fail to deliver genuine transformation. These fixes are a massive part of the problem with divorce rates today.

You are the catalyst in creating a positive, supportive environment. It begins with self-leadership, which is leading yourself with integrity and intention. Doing so sets a standard for your interactions and the overall tone of your relationship.

"Remember, you cannot lead your wife if you cannot first lead yourself."

Adopting this approach creates a more loving and respectful relationship and contributes to a healthier, more emotionally fulfilling environment. This is the essence of authentic leadership in a relationship marked by partnership, not control.

Chores

Chores often become a bargaining chip in relationships, especially among men who believe that "helping" more around the house will make their wives less tired, more amiable, and consequently more loving. "Hey, honey, I did the dishes. I did the laundry. I tidied up the living room." These statements may seem helpful, but they only attempt to get your wife to notice you and tell you how good you are. It's like saying, "I did good; can I have a cookie!?" There is a huge difference between being helpful and being involved. We will talk more about that in depth in Man at Home.

The common misstep here is treating household help like a transaction—expecting a reward for participation. You're like a child looking for a cookie for good behavior. Responsibilities at home should never be performed with the expectation of a reward. You're an adult; maintaining your living space should be a given, regardless of your marital status. If you don't heed my advice, you will when you're single.

"You're not getting a cookie; certainly, not her 'cookie.'"

Your wife likely sees your 'help' as something she would have done anyway. After a long day, often extending beyond your return from work well into the night as she manages both home and childcare, her perspective is not filled with gratitude but exhaustion. She keeps score in her mind and begins to feel like she's caring for another child rather than having a lover or a partner. Many women tell Kathryn and me, "My gosh, I'm his freaking mom." It's important to understand that this type of environment has no room for mad passion.

You must transition from just 'helping' to being genuinely involved. It's your house, too, and you need to be an adult and do your share of the day-to-day household duties—no matter how much you work or how much money you make. When you do this, don't expect a reward, a "Good boy," or anything else, especially sex or love. In a real marriage, it isn't about filling roles or ticking boxes; it's about being an active and proactive member of your household.

"This is especially true if your wife also works."

We will explore transforming these duties from chores to shared responsibilities in Man at Home and Man with Kids. The focus will be on breaking the traditional mindsets and creating a partnership where duties are shared equitably, enhancing respect and appreciation between you.

I Give

Many self-help and relationship resources miss the point regarding giving, leading to detrimental relationship practices. These sources typically discuss giving in the context of tangible items like flowers, cards, sticky notes, and jewelry. However, this surface-level advice misses the essential component of the intent behind the act of giving.

Dr. Robert Glover's No More Mr. Nice Guy talks about the problematic nature of giving with expectations that he calls "covert contracts." Here, the giver silently expects something in return, creating a dynamic where affection is transactional. "You are writing a covert contract, saying, 'If I do this for you, you need to do this for me,'" and this approach can lead to feelings of resentment and manipulation.

Many women have expressed discomfort with this dynamic on my social media platforms, likening it to feeling like a commodity or even a prostitute within their marriages. "I feel so used" is a common sentiment among those receiving such transactions. Many women confess, "I'm nothing but an object for his pleasure." Kathryn was no exception. When I would talk about "loving" her, she often replied, "You don't even like me." She felt this way because, in her mind, she could never live up to my expectations.

True giving should never be about what you get in return. Saying, "I love you," or offering a compliment, or any act of service should never be given with an expectation of attention or affection in response. This is also true for showing gratitude, spending quality time, or even physical touch. Of course, you will have intention behind the 'moves' you make, but if your giving is genuine, you will receive it naturally. Giving should express genuine affection and respect for your wife, not a strategy to secure her love or gratitude. Often, giving is sacrificial, yet you will feel grateful. We will use this to move you around the track faster in Man with Purpose and, later, using Momentum.

"Most men say I love you, just to hear it back."

As we move forward, it's crucial to rethink how we view and practice giving in relationships, ensuring that our actions genuinely appreciate and value our wife rather than fulfill our needs or desires.

"She will pour into you more than you ever knew you needed, when you give to her without expectations."

Ego Feeding

Checking your ego involves more than just showing integrity—it's about being truthful and authentic, qualities often glossed over in many resources.

Let's consider a scenario: You and your wife are watching a TV show, or you're at the fair, and she calls attention to another woman saying, "Wow, that woman's ass is hot." You respond with, "Oh yeah, but your ass is so much hotter." It might seem like you're complimenting her, but it's just appeasement if it's not genuine. Your wife is not dumb; she knows her body and is better aware of her appearance than anyone.

Even if your wife is a 10, being honest rather than saying what you think she wants to hear is essential. Your wife is likely never happy with her body and is consciously aware of her imperfections and insecurities. Pretending or exaggerating can feel disrespectful because it comes off as insincere. It also undermines the notion of being a Man at Play and a man with integrity who doesn't need to resort to placating to make his wife feel secure.

Being authentic means acknowledging truths, such as agreeing, "Yeah, Babe. She does have a nice bum," if that's what you genuinely think. The reaction this honesty may provoke in your wife—whether jealousy, insecurity, or anger—is secondary to maintaining your integrity.

As we explore in Man with Impact, handling the aftermath of such honesty involves using a STAT Response to navigate her reactions effectively, emphasizing that integrity and authenticity should govern your interactions, not your fear of response or the desire to please.

The Deeper Issue:

Ego feeding involves inflating one's ego. For example, making offhand remarks about potential attractions elsewhere, such as "I could have her if I wanted," when mentioning another woman, not only demonstrates a lack of control but also highlights a deficiency in self-worth.

There is no lasting advancement in boosting your own ego. If you succeed in making your wife jealous or insecure, negative anxiety or fear will not create an environment for the Peace Pillar. It's impossible to lift her into the life you want when you undermine the very need you assume you are lifting her toward.

The Talk

Talking with your wife, or having "the talk," is often recommended as the go-to solution by society and experts, pretty much everyone in life. You hear phrases like "Communication is key" or "Don't go to bed angry." However, this is where most will fail, exemplified by comments I see on social media: "I tried talking to my wife, and you know, I just don't understand why she doesn't have sex with me." This continuous emphasis on communication fails to recognize the core issue—you can't just talk problems away without the right skills.

"Just because you can string words together doesn't mean you know how to communicate."

The problem is more than just the act of talking; it's your lack of practical communication skills. Without these, you're not solving problems; you're exacerbating them. You think you're making progress, but without establishing a genuine connection, these are just superficial, first-order changes. They improve things temporarily, but soon, you're back where you started or deteriorate further.

You've seen this before. You have the 'talk,' and things get better for a while. At first, your sex life picks up. It doesn't take long to return to where it was, or worse. If you're already at the stage where sex is negligible to nonexistent, you can be a loud and clear voice to men with expectations and lose their power in Lords.

"Stop trying to talk your way into your wife's head, heart, and vagina."

Many men find themselves in a loop of trying to manipulate their way into their wife's affections—aiming for her head, her heart, or even her libido—without understanding that they are pushing her further away. You defend your needs, unload your feelings, and expect her to fix the issues. This approach doesn't create a safe space for her; it builds walls between you.

Your wife wants to be heard, but more than that, she needs a man who can handle her emotions and provide a secure environment where she feels valued and understood. Asking her how to fix things puts pressure on her, making her feel undervalued and overwhelmed. Remember, you once knew how to meet her needs—before the stress and strain of marriage blurred your abilities.

"You cannot be a Man in Power, taking responsibility while asking her what she needs to fix or relying on her to tell you how."

Sex is the biggest issue the 'talk' is used for; however, we'll discuss others later. Sex is simply the easiest example. She knows she should desire you and be eager to connect, but if she's merely going through the motions—what I call "job sex"—then it's not fulfilling for either of you. It's a chore for her, a box to tick, which only deepens your disconnect.

The solution isn't more talking. Foundationally, it's learning how to communicate effectively. It's about transforming ineffective talks into meaningful conversations that create connection and understanding. This means stepping back, assessing how you approach these discussions, and learning the skills necessary to structure the direction for the outcome.

"You're better off not talking for 30 days, acquiring the skills, practicing with Lords in my program, and then letting organic conversations begin with your wife again."

Stop relying on societal norms that tell you to talk more. Instead, focus on developing the ability to converse in a way that respects both your needs and hers, creating a deeper connection that moves beyond mere words. Follow my guidance to shift from superficial communication to meaningful interaction that truly addresses the heart of your relationship challenges. A word of caution: we'll discuss the timing of your feelings and needs in Man with Impact.

"Structure is future-oriented conversations and adventure; not communicating about, or playing, in the past or pain."

Yes Man

The familiar mantra "happy wife, happy life" has probably contributed to you becoming a Yes Man. Most of you will struggle with this more than you realize. You will learn the skills in The Reset but may find yourself continuing to appease and placate your wife, afraid to upset her.

You're subconsciously staying a few cars back rather than using the draft to take the lead. This approach is ineffective and prevents you from displaying the integrity, core values, and authenticity required of a leader. It's time to shift from following to leading.

"Happy wife, happy life is absolute bullshit."

Consider a simple scenario: your wife asks, "Would you like chicken or pasta for dinner?" If you respond based on what's easiest for her to make, like saying, "Yeah, pasta," you're missing a leadership opportunity. If you crave a steak, express that desire. If she points out there's no steak at home, you might say, "K, I'll be right back," and take the kids with you to get it. This shows initiative, decision-making, and partnership.

Many men struggle with making decisions because they fear their wife's disapproval or reaction. By making her the decision-maker for both of you, they inadvertently increase her burden. You become another child she must manage, not a partner she can rely on.

For instance, a client I worked with recently made a significant change by starting to decide what's for dinner without deferring to his wife. Within a week, his wife texted him: "It's only been a week of you making decisions and telling me what to make for dinner, and I don't want to punch you in the face anymore." This is a real example of how taking charge can alleviate the pressure on your wife and transform the dynamics of your relationship.

"You go on about your love language being physical touch. This makes sense to me. You really work hard to get her to punch you in the face."

When your wife asks what she should wear, "The blue or the red one?" don't shy away from answering. Choose assertively. Compliment her on her appearance in your preferred choice, like, "I like how the blue one hangs on your hips, Babe." Your genuine input can make a substantial difference. As a Man at Play, you'll learn to say something before she asks.

Making your own decisions is crucial for a man of value. When you hesitate or defer, you not only frustrate your wife but also turn her off by your indecisiveness. You must stop acting like a dependent child and start being the man she needs.

This book is designed to cut through the noise of simplistic advice like "happy wife, happy life" and guide you towards being your true self. It will empower you and your wife to be unapologetically yourselves and set the stage for a thriving relationship. When you begin engaging authentically, you will race toward the checkered flag together.

"The marriage you both signed up for."

Aha Moments:

"Aha" Moments are those light bulb moments that should click when you see them. The simple yet impactful changes you can make immediately. These are behaviors that many men unknowingly exhibit, which inadvertently drive their wives away and solidify the barriers between them. Recognizing and rectifying these habits can dramatically change the atmosphere of your home and create a more positive, welcoming environment—effectively creating the Green Light.

Think of these changes as what I call the "Second or Third Date Principle." Ask yourself: would your wife want to go on a second or third date with you if you exhibited these behaviors on the first or second date? For many of you, the concept of dating your wife may seem distant; you're not currently engaging in the kind of dates that create deep, intimate connections. This will change in Man at Play.

To emerge as a Lord in your relationship, these Aha Moments are where you start. They represent the initial steps out of the rut, positioning you to overtake the pace car eventually. By eliminating these basic turn-offs, you clear the path for more genuine and impactful interactions, allowing you to rev your engine and accelerate towards a more fulfilling marriage.

"They really are light bulb moments."

Cleanliness, Hygiene, and Manscaping:

I'm baffled by how often basic hygiene eludes many men. It's crucial to remember, especially as you age, that body odor gets worse.

"That's why they call it Grandpa Smell."

If your job is physically demanding and leaves you grimy, the first thing you should do when you get home is take a shower. Don't be perplexed by your wife's lack of interest if you skip this step.

Women, in general, associate smells with good things and bad. Think about how businesses market scents—perfumes, candles, lotions, essential oils—to women. Your smell matters. If you're unclean, don't expect your wife to be attracted to you physically or even want to engage intimately.

Poor hygiene doesn't just limit your chances of physical intimacy; it hampers basic interactions. Let me be frank: even though I don't work a physically demanding job anymore, I get dirty playing with my kids or working around the house. And yes, my feet can reek after a long day. I always make sure to clean up and smell fresh for Kathryn, so she isn't turned off.

It's not just about taking a quick shower. Proper grooming is essential. It's about comprehensive grooming—flossing, brushing, manscaping, haircuts, and skincare.

"No woman is sleeping with Freddy Krueger, Cousin It, or Jaws."

Let's put it this way: if you turned up to your first date smelling off, with crazy hair and dirty teeth, would there be a second date? Doubtful. You'd look like a sleazy salesperson, not a Ferrari—more like a wrecked Ford Focus that nobody wants to buy. Cleanliness, hygiene, and grooming are not optional; they are essential to making a good impression and must be addressed immediately.

Farting and Pooping:

What in the world? Who's pooping with the door open? Unfortunately, many of you are, and frankly, it's disgusting. If you're not one of those, great, but let's talk about farting—this is getting way out of control. Consider how simple it is to leave the room or wait until you're alone to let one rip. If your wife is in the car with you, don't trap her with the smell; step out first or ensure it dissipates before bringing her into a stench-filled space.

When your relationship is strong, a slip is easily overlooked, but if it's on rocky grounds, these habits can seriously degrade her respect and attraction towards you. I know some of you find it funny, and maybe your wife does too, on occasion. However, consistent disregard for where and when you fart can ruin intimacy. No one wants to go down under the covers after being subjected to a "Dutch Oven."

"You think she wants to put her mouth in the vicinity of that smell?"

Think about the example you're setting for your children. Why would you fart openly in front of your daughters or teach your son that it's acceptable? It's unlikely you'd behave this way at a business meeting, and you shouldn't be doing it in church, either. Let's face it; you know it. That's why you hope no one knows it was you. Why normalize it at home?

Eliminating (easy) Automatic Turn-Offs is crucial. If you're serious about maintaining a healthy relationship with your wife and family, start by controlling where and when you fart. Change your habits consistently, whether you're with friends or alone. This isn't just about avoiding embarrassment—it's about respecting your family's space and creating a more respectful and intimacy-inducing environment.

Dressing For Success:

Think about the best-dressed man in the room. Everyone is talking to him. His suit looks trim, and he exudes respect and confidence. If you want to rekindle intimacy and earn back respect, a significant way to inspire this is through your choice of attire. Dressing for success not only commands respect but also uplifts your spirit and that of your wife. You dress sharply for meetings or dates, so why not elevate your home attire on occasion, too?

Once, Kathryn mentioned she liked a specific pair of my underwear, and embarrassingly, I wore that same pair for seven days straight. That was not only foolish but also a hygiene failure. This highlights the importance of dressing appropriately, especially when you're feeling low. Reflect back on your first date — if you had shown up looking like a slob, would she have been eager for a second date?

That doesn't mean you can't relax in comfortable clothes at home but choose well-fitting, neat casual wear. For example, I sometimes swap my home attire between comfy sweats and jeans, and then maybe a pair of Lululemon dress pants that are equally comfortable but look sharp. This variety shows that you care about how you present yourself, impacting how your wife perceives you. You are also breaking free of the 'same old' she's used to seeing.

Avoid lounging in just any old ratty sweats, backward caps, or faded shirts and jerseys just because they're cozy. Just like technology, your wardrobe needs an upgrade. If you continually appear well-put-together, it signals to your wife that you value yourself and, by extension, value her and your relationship.

"Think about the impression you want to leave: a sharp, 4K, high-definition presence versus a fuzzy, 480p."

A Gentleman:

At a minimum, you should consistently use "please" and "thank you". It's surprising how manners have deteriorated. At our twins' birthday party, which had 80 attendees, I observed numerous men receive slices of pizza from their wives without pausing their conversations even to offer a simple "Thank You." They provided no acknowledgment—no smile, no small gesture of appreciation, just grab and ignore.

Reflect on this: How often does your "Thank you" sound disinterested? "Please" should convey respect, and "Thank you" should express true gratitude. If you're aiming for a respectful partnership with your wife or you seek to respect yourself, these small gestures of chivalry are foundational.

Being a gentleman means showing respect, which is inherently manly and considerate. Consider the meaning of "Gentleman"—it's revealing. Beyond the basics, you can embrace more grand gestures similar to those seen in movies. I love to carry Kathryn over puddles, which always ends up being a fun, if not a slightly precarious, moment. Sometimes, we slip, and I catch us both. In her eyes, these acts enhance my manliness. We laugh together, turning a potentially scary moment into delightful fun—a Man at Play.

Understand your wife's preferences. For instance, I don't pull Kathryn's chair out or help her into her jacket, as she prefers that I not touch her hair. Yet, simpler acts like grabbing her a drink when I get one for myself are effortless and coincide with basic courtesies like saying "please" and "thank you." Opening the car door for her is another significant gesture of respect and care. There are countless ways to show your respect, honor, love, and cherish your wife, beginning with the simple yet profound act of being a gentleman.

Making decisions:

We will discuss this more in several chapters of this book, but I wanted to bring this in quickly. Elaborating on Society's Solutions and making decisions relates to a very powerful light bulb and is crucial to regaining the leadership role in your home.

Remember I talked about your wife feeling like she has another child? She must plan the schedules for everything. When you start making more decisions and letting your wife begin to challenge those decisions, you will be in a much better place. In Man with Impact, you will learn how to respond when your wife is not on board with your decisions.

For now, start answering the question when she gives it to you. Which do you want? What do you want? Where do you want to go? Start there. That's the most important thing you can do. At a minimum, become hyper-aware of how stupid you look when you can't decide what you want for dinner or where you are going after the football game. Give two options after cheer practice with the kids to avoid looking stupid. "OK, Fam, Dairy Queen for blizzards or McDonald's for burgers?"

You should always play an active role instead of looking uninterested. A lot of times, you won't care. Your wife might text you, "What do you want to do on Friday night?" And you might mean it when you say, "I don't care, Babe, whatever.", but your wife does care. She feels alone and disconnected and wonders about her life choices. Consequently, she feels like you are not her partner. If you are not a partner, you can never rebuild your connection, never mind lead your wife.

Lecturing vs. Pillow Talk:

I've already cautioned you about trying to talk your way into your wife's head, heart, and vagina, but I want to emphasize a point now about lecturing. Isn't pillow talk much more appealing? At my worst, I was giving three and seven-day lectures on why she should want me, how to love and respect me, and the rules of marriage. How often have you done this?

I'm sure you don't remember much intimacy following those drawn-out, often one-sided, arguments. Remember, you married an intelligent woman because she was exactly that—an intelligent woman. If you think you've 'married down' intellectually, then you're probably lecturing more than you realize. Your wife doesn't need your mental prowess.

Change your approach. Your wife might just be looking to discuss a problem or even vent a little, not get a solution shoved in her face. You're probably overreacting out of defensiveness because you feel inadequate or are desperate for her approval, which leads to these lectures.

"Nice Guys like to fix things to solve problems to keep the peace, really, to prove they are great men."

Sometimes, this isn't purposeful, and you may not realize that you are doing this. Many men really can't stand that their wives are hurting. They want to fix the situation. You more than likely do this with your kids, too. When you can't fix it, it hurts. It makes you feel like you're not good enough to save the day—-not good enough in any way.

"This amplifies when you need to fix the issue just to stop another bad night from happening."

Instead of lecturing your wife, if she asks, "What time is it?" give her a straightforward answer: "It's four o'clock." Don't spiral into overthinking her motives or crafting elaborate responses like, "Oh, the clock was made in England in 1912, survived a shipwreck in 1946. We're just lucky the watch is here. The boat was blue..." and so on. Eventually, you're talking about unrelated issues like the color of watch straps. These kinds of reactions stem from anxiety and insecurity, causing you to over-explain and inadvertently start lecturing.

"You are 100% worried if you are in trouble. Did you forget what you were supposed to do? Did you say you'd do something by a certain time? Is the whole night ruined? I don't want another fight. Is sex off the table again?"

Blame arises out of frustration anytime a conversation turns negative. You may start bringing up past issues or even things from the past that are irrelevant. You start to recall every detail of anything that comes to mind in the argument but miss the emotional connection. "You didn't specify if you wanted a gold or black watch. Last time, you got me socks anyway. I even remembered you liked rose gold straps with diamonds... You don't care about what I want." We'll talk about reality checks later.

See, communicating or, better, a conversation is never about lecturing; it's about connecting. You don't need to sleep on the couch or use the 'D' word to solve your problems. Instead, aim for lighter, more playful interactions as part of being a Man at Play, where you can engage in meaningful yet fun conversations without the pressure of fixing everything.

Using Wit as a Weapon or Using It for Good:

This topic is not discussed enough in resources, likely because many will dispute my stance, especially those who enjoy sarcasm—I certainly do, and perhaps so does your wife. You might already engage in playful banter, picking on each other humorously. It's understandable why this might seem fun and acceptable, something you're used to doing, even with your buddies.

However, women often experience emotions more intensely, and they can fluctuate rapidly. Imagine having a perfect day only to unintentionally wound your wife with what you thought was a harmless joke. Such comments can come across as condescending, demeaning, or hurtful, even if that wasn't your intention—or perhaps it was, on a subconscious level.

I remember one night, while we were getting ready to change our daughters' diapers for bed (during a good phase in our relationship), Kathryn forgot to bring the diapers upstairs with her. When she said, "Oh, I forgot them," I snapped with wit, "Ah, Super Mom strikes again," before running down to get them myself.

At that moment, my attempt at humor, intended to push (perhaps?) who was the better parent, fell flat. Earlier that day, Kathryn had been harsh with our daughter Briar, and by evening, she was still feeling guilty about her reaction. My sarcastic comment only deepened her reflection, turning what should have been a Green Light into a glaring red, ruining our night. It highlighted that I still had much to learn about providing structure and leading positively.

Wit should never be used as a potential weapon. Here's how you can pivot it towards something positive: Another time, Kathryn misplaced her phone on our way to church. She admitted, "Oh, I forgot my phone." I could have made a biting remark like, "Typical of you," since she regularly misplaces her phone and coffee mug—daily used items—potentially making her feel worse, especially since she might worry about being unavailable for a woman in crisis. Instead, I chose a lighter touch, saying, "I'm with who I want to be with," which brought a smile to her face and a squeeze of my hand in agreement.

"This has been an inside 'line,' not joke, for years now."

Using wit as a weapon, particularly with your wife, rarely ends well. Instead, using wit for good to uplift and brighten anyone's day is invariably the more rewarding choice. Your wife is obviously the most rewarding place to practice this; your children should be a strong second.

"You miss 100% of the shots you don't take."

She's Not Using Sex as a Weapon:

Imagine your wife is automatically repulsed by you, and you've come to realize that it's your actions—pushing her away from meaningful conversations, playful flirting, genuine dates—that are to blame. In this case, your lack of intimacy is not her using sex as a weapon; rather, it's a result of your behavior.

"Kathryn told me she was repulsed by me."

Even if you're dealing with a highly confrontational situation where your wife explicitly refuses sex for specific reasons, recognize that this isn't her using sex as a weapon. You become the weapon when you refuse to acknowledge and address your contributions to the problem.

"You can do it right all day long and then snap at the kids… You're the weapon."

Consider the parallels with other forms of conflict, like walking away from an argument, name-calling, or threatening divorce—as I did all the time—telling Kathryn I wanted a divorce and reinforcing my point by sleeping on the couch. These reactions are the same as her saying she doesn't want to be intimate. If you've made bad choices, take responsibility. We all fail. I certainly have, and I will again. The same is true for you. Our goal should be to continuously strive towards being our best selves.

Your wife also needs understanding and patience during these times. If you want patience, lead with it. Some of you won't relate because your marriage isn't as severe, but this principle still applies even to scenarios of job, pity, or fear sex where intimacy is more about duty than desire.

If she's just having sex as a commitment, as Kathryn did for a period, then it's clear that sex is not being used as a weapon but rather as a strained attempt to uphold vows or keep you happy and regulate your emotions to keep the peace. By understanding this, we can work towards creating mad passion in your relationship, ensuring that intimacy is mutually satisfying and genuinely about connection from both of you.

Stop The Pics, Pokes and Peeps:

Acting like a horny teenager, sending pictures of your penis, and poking at or making childish gestures at her genitalia takes a neon flashing "open" sign and turns it into a glaring red light. Women do not like this behavior, and they prefer to be imaginative when it comes to seeing our bodies. Even if this seemed to have had a positive impact before, it's time to stop. I used to say, "Peep," and touch Kathryn, poke her whenever I was ready, and grab her hand and place it on me when I had an erection.

Like a child, I sent a ton of pics. None of this was attractive to her. None of it turned her on. Now, this 'gesturing' in my past is a running joke whenever we're out with a new couple. In Kathryn's program—The White Picket Fence Project—it would be easy for women to spiral down a path and laugh about their husbands for this behavior. In both of our programs, we shut down the negativity of such things.

What if It Was Your Daughter?:

Imagine if your daughter approached you, distress written across her face, and confessed, "I have sex with him, but I don't want to, EVER". As a father, your blood should boil, and your protective instincts should flare. Whether you once acted like I did or not, you would forcefully advise her against it. You'd explain that she doesn't have to give in, detailing the respect and care she rightfully deserves in any relationship, especially her husband.

Apply the same thought process as a husband. If your wife reluctantly engages in intimacy of any kind or feels pressured during those moments—as I regrettably pressured and, at times, guilted or forced Kathryn in the past—then it's essential to reflect. If such actions were directed towards your daughter, would you stand by? No. A Man with Kids would be in a fury, advocating for her right to refuse.

"Should you start looking over your shoulder for her father?"

This book will dive into everything your wife deserves in your marriage, highlighting that meeting her needs is not just about getting what you want but genuinely uplifting her unapologetic self—the real her. Whether you're a Christian or hold other beliefs, understand that a truly loving relationship requires mutual respect and fulfillment. Meet your wife's needs, and in turn, she'll meet yours.

Stop Using Coping Mechanisms:

It is crucial to stop using coping mechanisms immediately. These are often related to addiction, or at least they can be treated as such. They're methods we use to handle life's hardships, and while coping may seem helpful, it ultimately undermines your full potential. Coping mechanisms keep you stagnant, preventing progress in life and damaging your relationships. We will cover this in Man with Impact and your SAFE Reactions; keeping yourself safe, rather than protecting your wife, family, and future.

"You will learn a lot about this and its relevance in Morrow Momentum. Stay tuned."

I urge men who join my program to openly discuss their coping mechanisms and addictions right from the start. In Man in Control, I will outline a plan to help you overcome these issues by recognizing and addressing them head-on. I encourage you to reach out for support through our online resources at https://MorrowMarriage.com/Tools. There, you'll find a wealth of resources, support from mentors, other Lords, and personal guidance from Kathryn, me and our mentors.

Using coping mechanisms to deal with problems, rather than confronting them directly, sets you up for failure. It affects how you view yourself and how your wife sees you, pushing her further away and adding bricks to the wall between you. You eliminate opportunities for intimate connections.

"Remember, you cannot lead your wife if you cannot first lead yourself."

If you find yourself reliant on any coping mechanisms, it's time to replace strong habits with stronger skills. Retrain your brain, rewire your nervous pathways, and truly reach your goals. Although we will address the how-to later, you can start by identifying the common coping mechanisms that you use and addressing them effectively.

Addressing Porn, Masturbation, and Infidelity:

One of men's go-to coping mechanisms is porn, masturbation and infidelity. Stop immediately. Recognize that these actions train your brain in ways that undermine your roles as a husband, father, and leader. Embracing pornography or engaging in affairs, whether they're physical or emotional, is a betrayal of your commitment to your wife. It's impossible to say you desire a genuine connection with your wife while engaging in behaviors that fundamentally betray her trust. This includes seemingly minor actions like casual chats with women online or getting a visual 'fix' on social media.

Justifying these behaviors as a need for "release" only further burdens your marriage. These actions set expectations and demands on your wife that smother her. Once you achieve the kind of meaningful and fulfilling sex life I prescribe—the checkered flag—you'll find you no longer crave these destructive habits. It's crucial to see these actions for what they are: betrayals.

Pornography not only damages your perception of healthy sexual relationships but also affects your physical responses and can lead to significant psychological issues. The problems often start young, with many men carrying shame from having to hide their habits since childhood.

For those struggling, help is available. One of our Lords offers an effective porn recovery program, and Lords, in general, are unashamed to help you in this area. They have been where you are. Similarly, the principles in Destin Gerek's book, The Evolved Masculine, or his course, are excellent for developing self-awareness around these negative issues caused by a reaction to porn use.

This is about more than just stopping your need for release. It's about seeking help and building a new pathway forward. Engage with support systems like the ones offered through our community at https://MorrowMarriage.com/tools, where you can find resources and peer support to overcome these challenges.

"Keep in mind, I'm not about your giving up your daily 'release', I'm all about getting the release with your wife that sets you free."

Consider starting with short, manageable challenges, such as going seven days, then 14, and eventually 30 days without pornography, and build from there. This approach mirrors the support structure of programs like Alcoholics Anonymous, where having someone to call—a sponsor—can make all the difference. It's about taking actionable steps toward recovery and reclaiming the respect, integrity, and closeness you wish to have in your marriage.

"As you work through The Reset, and with the support of Lords, mindsets will shift, and much of the work is done for you, believe it or not."

Alcohol, Drugs, and Substance Abuse:

Alcohol and drugs are normal in society, but as I learned the hard way, they can ruin your life. Once, Kathryn suggested we go to our pastor's Halloween party, but I stayed behind drinking all day and night. I missed out on life and the direction I truly wanted for myself. Even if your wife drinks, you must lead by example.

"You're not just stuck in a pit stop; you're missing the entire event."

Kathryn and I believe that cutting out alcohol earlier could have shortened our struggles by at least two years. Remember, while there's a place for moderate (or safe) drinking, right now might not be the time for any at all, especially if you're working on becoming a Man with Impact, mastering emotional control, and adopting my response versus reaction training.

"Quit drinking. Alcohol brings out the parts of you that you've done little or no work on. That guy can't save his marriage."

Video Games, Social Media, and TV:

Social media was crucial in connecting many of you with my teachings, and for that, I'm grateful. However, it's now time to reduce these distractions. We will explore focusing techniques in Man with Purpose. Currently, these entertainment forms are preventing you from achieving your goals, often serving as excuses for why you're too tired or busy. If you're going to use social media, from now on, only use it to learn. Don't waste time with distractions.

Some men know more about sports stats or fake news on social media than their wives. They have more information about the drama of others than their own marriages. It's time to cut down on-screen time and start living in the real world, engaging in activities that truly enrich your life and legacy. Man with Purpose and Momentum will help you with proper social media use. When you do it my way, it will blow your mind.

Venting:

Venting or complaining with friends, engaging in anger binges, or chasing insecurity might feel gratifying at the moment, but they actually trap you in a negative cycle. Reflect on how you're dealing with problems—often, it's through harmful discussions that only reinforce your struggles. You seek validation from others because you don't like how you feel.

You are playing the victim to gain sympathy, avoiding taking responsibility for your own actions and choices. You do this even when you go ask for help to solve the problem(s). This attitude has no place in a life aimed at growth and improvement in any area.

"When you are married, you are betraying your wife."

It's astonishing how many professionals, like therapists, advise ending relationships too quickly. I've seen an alarming 70% of men in my program who have hired therapists are suggested to leave their wives, use pornography, and sometimes even recommend open relationships. Shockingly, during a group call in a program I was in, the program creator and coach once referred to a client's wife as a "Fucking bitch"—a clear example of how not to lead or set an example.

Bitching and moaning with friends and family or trolling on social media to justify yourself or discredit your wife does not move you forward. It only sinks you deeper into your justifications as to why you deserve better. Reflect deeply: You succeed in every area of your life when you surround yourself with positive support, and you fail in areas where you blame others. Actions that create forward momentum are key, not those fixed in contempt and blame.

"At a mastermind with two of my mentors, Cole DaSilva: @coleluisdasilva and Brian Mark: @therealbrianmark reminded us, 'proximity is what takes you where you want to go.' Like in

business, if you surround yourself with the right people, your relationship will thrive."

In Lord's sessions, we focus on real actions—those that create actual change and personal accountability, not those that allow you to coast through life or promote failure. This is about seizing control and not surrendering to the negative influences or easy escapes. My approach sets the foundation for becoming a Man in Power. As a Man in Power, coping mechanisms are replaced with constructive habits that propel you toward your goals and a fulfilled life.

"I cannot wait to introduce you to Morrow Momentum. You will never play in your pain again."

Workaholics:

Loving your work is commendable, but it can also lead you down a path of endless busyness, distracting you from what truly matters—your purpose, legacy, and family. Often, work becomes a coping mechanism, a way to avoid confrontations and challenges in personal life. I've been there; there were years when I would see Kathryn only sparingly as I buried myself in work to sidestep our arguments. It's important to understand that this avoidance is akin to running away or shutting down.

As we will explore in SAFE Reactions, avoidance is a form of self-preservation. Many men, perhaps unknowingly, sidestep their marital responsibilities or dodge parts of this program that are uncomfortable. However, real change demands facing these challenges head-on. You cannot hide behind your work or bypass what you think is not right for you.

"Learn to do what you can't, don't do what you can, and you will be unstoppable."

True responsibility involves acknowledging and owning up to these issues now. It's about becoming a true Man in Power, moving beyond mere coping mechanisms which, let's be clear, never equate to success. Instead, they represent only coasting, settling for things in life you do not want. Set your sights on accomplishing the goals laid out, harness your vibrant, life-giving energy, and channel it into building something magnificent. Share this enhanced life with the world, especially with your wife.

Maintaining Power:

It's critical to embody what it means to be a Man in Power. Let me be clear: Do not play in your pain. Turning to social media, Reddit, or Facebook groups that validate your sense of victimization won't aid your growth. These platforms should serve as springboards for rising above, not for settling.

Consider the amount of time spent on wasted conversations. Don't use anyone in your life, including my Lords chats or Zoom calls, to focus on the faults of your wife rather than constructive solutions. Any conversations you have should be used as opportunities to seek advice on reframing your thoughts and complaints toward being productive. Remember the reasons behind your decision to change and use that motivation to persist and push through challenges.

Remember, it takes two to tango but only one to lead. If you're not leading, you're not dancing the tango—you're doing the chicken dance while your wife does the Macarena. While most will suggest finding a new dance partner, this often stems from a reluctance to take the lead themselves.

"It does not take two; it takes one to lead."

Seek out support that challenges you to rethink your approach. You are working to change deep and ingrained behaviors, so when you face failure, you will need to reframe your perspective. Instead of blaming your wife, just ask yourself: What could I be doing differently? How have my actions contributed to our current situation? Understanding your role in this process will transform your approach and provide paths to heal your relationship.

"In a low, I don't take trails, I blaze 'em."

Releasing Your Wife:

The final step in embracing full responsibility and embodying a Man in Power involves the most difficult part for many men: releasing your wife from the hurt she has caused you. This entails forgiving her for actions, both significant and minor, that have caused you resentment.

Understand that she, like you, are reacting based on deep-seated programming, and your actions have likely influenced some of her behaviors. It drives me crazy when people push for leaving your wife and divorce or criticize her actions without understanding the big picture. Remember, both of you have been shaped by your upbringing and further modified these behaviors as a couple.

"If you need to change, you're not the real you. That means she's not the real her."

Consider the common "red flags" that make people consider leaving their wives. It's crucial to acknowledge your part in raising these flags, just as your wife has influenced your behaviors. By accepting responsibility, you break the cycle of blame and pave the way for true forgiveness.

You have decades of happiness ahead of you in a reciprocal relationship where she expresses genuine curiosity about your feelings.

You are building the foundation of that future on her freedom to feel with no fear of your reactions - not your continued bad habits. This step involves understanding that her actions, whether shutting down, yelling, having an affair, leaving you, or even abusing, are part of a bigger picture that you were involved in creating.

"I don't care if she kicks you in the balls. You allowed it to go this far."

Reflect on the reasons behind your frustrations. Why do you feel disrespected? Is it her infidelity, her disdain toward you, or has she filed for a divorce or a restraining order? Maybe she comes at you with a cold heart, or you haven't been intimate in months or years.

Ask yourself if these behaviors appeared suddenly or if they developed over time. You likely enabled their escalation. In the early days of your relationship, these problems were probably not there, but as disagreements led to shutdowns, passive or aggressive behaviors, and, eventually, contempt, these things were born.

For example, if your wife did cheat on you in the beginning, you're an idiot, and you really need this program. It's more than likely she did not. You need this program because you let her get to a level of disrespect, like cheating, by allowing your relationship to get this bad and go this far. That's on you.

You have a significant influence on your wife's actions and reactions. By assuming your responsibility, you can start steering the relationship in a new direction. This doesn't mean the issues are solely your fault, but focusing on what you can control—yourself—is key.

"If you could enable the negative to grow, you can now influence the positive."

Letting go is particularly challenging with infidelity, but understand it was a breakdown of needs being met, as displayed in John Gottman's Cascade of Betrayal, which lists precursors to an affair—many of which are actions you, more than likely, are responsible for. John and Julie Gottman are world-renowned marriage therapists, and Kathryn is Level III trained in their work.

"24 things happen leading up to an affair. Address her morals later. Who betrayed who first?"

Choose three or four deeply impactful issues and forgive her for them. For example, I had to forgive Kathryn for her harsh words, the lack of sexual connection, and her disrespect towards my role as a man. The most difficult for me was her having me arrested, charged with assault, and the restraining order that followed. Throughout this book, I dive into these issues in detail. You can better understand how to move forward by examining your role in these dynamics. If you're following this program, you might revisit these topics several times, comparing notes and reflecting on changes, as many do with The Reset.

Let me share a story. A Lord once considered quitting the program because his wife was involved in an affair. As the Cascade of Betrayal shows, affairs often stem from unmet needs. Consider who she feels safe with—if it's not you, she might look elsewhere.

This isn't about morals now; it's about recognizing your part in failing to meet her needs. Focus on your actions and their impact, such as how your insecurities might have contributed to her seeking comfort elsewhere. Ultimately, Corey decided to stay in the program and tackled these challenges head-on. After two months of living with the other man, his wife moved back home.

"We're like horny teenagers now."—Corey R. Canada.

I encourage you to do the same. Identify three things that deeply hurt you, discuss them with others who understand, and use this process to become a Man with Impact. Explore more tools and resources at https://MorrowMarriage.com/Tools to aid in this journey. This approach isn't just about handling infidelity; it applies to any struggle where you might feel victimized. By releasing the blame you hold, you empower yourself to move forward.

"Every time I thought about moving on, I reminded myself of the patience formula and recognized how long I've been showing up compared to how long I put my wife through Hell." —Greg Hedrick, USA: Mentor to Lords.

The Patience Formula:

Navigating difficult, toxic, or sexless marriages and creating growth within them often feels like an eternity. This realization led me to develop what I call The Patience Formula. Significant changes like shedding a hundred pounds or transforming a relationship don't happen overnight. Peace and a safe environment are mandatory. We will cover this later as you step into being a Man with Impact.

"I don't share this to deter you, rather to promote complete transparency."

Consider that no journey starts with full knowledge of the obstacles ahead. I don't know your wife personally, nor do I know the full extent of your situation. I know that both of you, influenced by a lifetime of experience, have evolved and changed. Your wife may resist change or leadership, much like Kathryn did. Kathryn certainly did not want a leader by the time I started showing up in our marriage, and she still doesn't (really) need one today. The effort you invest and the understanding you create will heavily influence the outcomes of your relationship.

"The Patience Formula isn't a mathematical equation. It's a concept to guide your patience levels."

Your Patience = (Length of Time × Pain / Wounds / Trauma) – Tolerance

Multiply the duration of the difficult times by the intensity of the pain, trauma, or wounds inflicted—considering both what you and your wife have endured. This includes reflecting on her past traumas and recognizing that they don't need to impact your current relationship directly; they may amplify the issues at hand. From there, subtract your tolerance for these hardships.

My own experience spanned four intense years filled with pain and trauma, lacking the insights and support systems that are now at your disposal through resources like the ones found at https://MorrowMarriage.com/Tools. My tolerance was low, but embracing my role as a Man in Power shifted my perspective to allow Kathryn space to express her feelings—a pivotal step that we will dive deeper into in Man with Impact.

Your experiences will vary. It's important to remain patient even if your wife exhibits behaviors that feel like personal attacks or sets boundaries by making plans with others that exclude you. These behaviors didn't appear suddenly; they're not the result of a simple switch being flipped. Make sure you look for small wins—improved communication, shared laughter, or increased intimacy. These are significant indicators that you're making progress.

Every lap you complete faster, every collision you avoid, and every repair you make counts as you run the race. Maybe you haven't had many meaningful conversations lately, yet now she's engaging more—

recognize that as a win. If your intimate moments were rare and are becoming more frequent, that doubles your connection.

So, let this guide your patience. Consistency is the key to transforming your marriage into a thriving partnership. Keep showing up and pushing forward, and remember, every small win is a step in the right direction. We'll explore more strategies in Man with Impact, but remember, becoming a Man in Power is about setting the pace, not just keeping up with her.

MAN WITH IMPACT

Communication is NOT key

Man with Impact

"This section had the biggest impact on me. When I learned about SAFE Reacting, to start understanding my wife, and what direction could look like based on the Three Types of Wives, I knew I was where I needed to be: The Reset."---Dave Waldman, USA: Mentor to Lords.

Now that you have the tools to be a Man in Power and have started taking ownership of the mistakes you made in your marriage, it's time to address a pivotal issue that is common in many relationships. Society misguided us as men, but as we tackle this issue, you will soon become a Man with Impact.

This step completes the Peace Pillar, opening the way for authenticity by creating a safe space in your relationship. This environment encourages your wife to fully open her heart, mind, and body to you, rekindling the intimacy you experienced at the beginning of your relationship.

"At the risk of my humility, Man with Impact is a fundamental piece missing from most books, programs, or what coaches will teach."

Trust is the key that opens the door to your emotional connection and will be expanded upon in upcoming pillars. This phase focuses on creating the Peace Pillar with communication tools that lead to conversation and genuine connection. These tools make heavy communication evolve into effortless conversations, and the idea that relationships require hard work begins to dissipate. Then, we look toward the future. Your wife must be on board and ready to embrace this new pace for this transition. You must lead the way.

"Communication is not key; the right communication skills are."

Man with Impact primarily aims to provide direction and structure, helping your wife feel secure enough to express her feelings and reconnect on a deeper level. I'll equip you with tools that facilitate showing love through understanding and support by ensuring she feels acknowledged and valued.

Our wives must feel this emotional bond, and you should desire this connection, too. As her steadfast "rock," "lighthouse," "shoreline," or "shoulder to cry on," you become indispensable in her journey of emotional recovery and intimacy rebuilding at every rung of the Rejection Ladder.

"The rock, lighthouse, shoreline, and shoulder to cry on… I didn't make that shit up; climb my Rejection Ladder."

This stage will be the most challenging for you if your wife is a coasting Type 3 or a Vicious Type 3. But you don't have to face this alone. In Lords, we leverage our collective experiences through my app, learning from each man's journey and the mentors available. Embrace your role with the power you have harnessed.

"Feminine feels. Feminine flows. Masculine loves her through it. Masculine provides structure and direction."

In becoming her protector again, you must regulate your emotions and allow hers to flow freely—whether they soar high or dive deep. The nuances of her femininity, conscious or not, shouldn't deter you. As a grounded, proud man, you recognize that while our stories may vary, the symptoms and solutions are the same.

By embodying your masculine strength and inner resilience as a Man in Power, you create the conditions for your wife to open up vulnerably. This is how you forge a lasting impact, providing the direction, structure, and safety she needs to engage in healing fully. This is how you rebuild trust in your relationship.

"She's going to run into the side of your car. Embrace it."

Look In The Mirror:

Men need to start looking in the mirror. Who are you? Are you even proud? Do you stare into your reflection and feel guilt? You justify your behaviors and ignore the shame because you don't know what you don't know.

"You should not be proud of yourself if you are emotionally deregulated, snap or shut down on your wife or children; there's nothing to justify."

Who's looking back at you now as you read this? You will never stop rising now. As you rise, you will break down the wall you've helped build between you and your wife. A Man with Impact embraces responsibility for shaping the communication and direction of your relationship. This sets the Peace Pillar, where our focus shifts from mere communication to thriving conversations.

"If you can handle your wife's rejection, you can take on the world."

John and Julie Gottman provide invaluable tools for rejection, although I've created my systems incorporating my interpretations of them. Though Kathryn is Gottman Level III trained, and neither of us is a licensed therapist, the principles we apply from their teachings are tailored to our systems. John Gottman identifies defensiveness, criticism, stonewalling, and contempt as the Four Horsemen of the Apocalypse—destructive behaviors that foreshadow divorce. Understanding these pitfalls is crucial.

These horsemen have influenced your behavior, and understanding this is essential because your triggers amplify defensive responses to perceived threats in every area of your life. This leads to other horsemen running wild. Dr. Glover's concept of the 'Nice Guy' highlights our tendency to seek approval through pleasing our wife, which is often at the expense of our own needs.

When our needs are unmet, we default to survival mode, manifesting behaviors such as defensiveness when faced with fundamental issues like your wife using her phone. If you misinterpret these actions, they can spiral out of control, preventing the possibility of a safe and secure environment.

Recognizing early signs of these threat-based reactions enables proactive management. For example, if your wife's casual conversation on her phone triggers insecurity, understanding this as a reflexive reaction helps you respond logically rather than impulsively. This awareness prevents all the negative emotions from cascading. This keeps you from spinning out on the track.

It's important to address deeper insecurities like feeling inadequate or unloved. These feelings feed our reactions and perpetuate cycles of anger and frustration. Acknowledging and confronting these insecurities allows you to break free from destructive patterns and focus on creating peace and impact.

"Insecurity is a monster. When it grips you, it will spin your brain in 19 different directions—all the wrong way."

When you sense a threat, your immediate step shouldn't be unraveling every detail but acknowledging your defensive stance. Recognizing this state helps you avoid escalating into more destructive behaviors like criticism, stonewalling, or contempt.

Contempt, in particular, strips you of your power rapidly, pushing you towards extreme reactions that undermine the New Man. Remember the potentially severe consequences of letting anger control your actions. I failed in this area during a fight that led to assault charges and a restraining order. Reflecting on these moments provides a sobering reminder of the importance of self-regulation.

"For years, I couldn't believe Kathryn called the cops. Now I see she wasn't safe enough to leave it alone. Not even we know what we're capable of in this state."

Understanding your typical response to stress helps you to manage your reactions. Are you more likely to withdraw or deal with a hard conversation? Are you like I was? Do you just lose control? Being fully aware of who you are is crucial for growth. As you prepare to adopt healthier behaviors, aligning your actions with the principles taught in the Reset will transform you into a Man with Impact, fully capable of creating the marriage you both signed up for.

"Better still to pull that woman out of your wife again."

SAFEREACTION

S

Sabotage – Am I sabotaging with my coping mechanisms?

A

Approval/Accountability – Am I doing this for approval or being held accountable for something I said I would do, should have done or should be doing?

F

Fight, Flight, Freeze, Fawn – Am I defaulting to my normal negative reaction?

E

Enforcing Boundaries – Am I enforcing boundaries that I probably won't even follow through on or am not in a position to even use?

SAFE Reactions: Explanation:

In this program, you will become the New "Man" I describe, yet, based on old habits, undermine your growth. You may initiate change, creating a Green Light, but quickly hit a red light by falling back into old habits. This typically happens through threat-based reactions, which prove your lack of progress and signal to your wife that the changes aren't real—reinforcing her disbelief.

When you finally stop shutting down, you puke your feelings or aggressively try to get what you want. This is why it's crucial to avoid what I refer to as SAFE Reactions. These reactions are not a sign of actual safety; instead, they are your programmed response to protect yourself from perceived threats.

Such reactions are often deeply ingrained, developed from childhood, and edited over time to work against your growth. When you engage in these reactions, you are not fighting for your relationship or your future; you are fighting for yourself.

"There goes your protector card."

To truly embody a Man with Impact, you must always take responsibility for what you can control. We cannot control our wives, their reactions, their personal growth, or how they've been programmed. We also can't do anything to rewind how we enabled negative programming. Our goal should be to knock the wall down, not reinforce it with SAFE Reactions.

"If you could influence the negative, you can influence the positive now."

SAFE reactions erode the emotional connection necessary for authentic change. They convince your wife to maintain her faith in the "old you" rather than believe in the New Man you were born to be. Reflect on how often your wife might feel overwhelmed, anxious, or threatened by your presence. This is a direct result of SAFE Reactions—all those times, you lost your power and blamed her for the disconnect between you.

"There is no way around it. You will blame push, shame dump, and guilt throw just to feel whole again."

To progress, we must first release these programmed, protective reactions. Learning to respond rather than react defensively is key to sustaining your changes. This shift is crucial for building trust and allowing you and your wife to connect genuinely and become unapologetically your most authentic selves again.

SAFE REACTIONS

S: is for Sabotage
A: is for Approval or Accountability
F: is for Fight, Flight, Freeze or Fawn
E: is for Enforcing boundaries

S: Sabotage

Am I sabotaging my future? We will explore this concept regarding how coping mechanisms undermine the New Man. These can include substance abuse, pornography, excessive work, social media, TV, sports, and more. Each of these not only consumes the time you could spend growing into the man you were born to be but also replaces genuine feelings of success with fleeting highs.

Take pornography, for instance. You might turn to it because you're not having sex (or quality sex) with your wife. She feels betrayed even if she doesn't know it—and, more likely, she does. This form of betrayal is because you're seeking pleasure from other women, which erodes the emotional connection with your wife, as discussed earlier. The damage goes beyond immediate effects, contributing to issues like ED and supporting disgusting industries like human trafficking.

Alcohol and drugs are another form of sabotage. Reflecting on my journey, I recognize how substance abuse added years of struggle for Kathryn and me. It doesn't just cloud judgment; it builds walls between you and your loved ones. If you were drunk and obnoxious on a first date today, would your wife choose to go out with you again? Probably not. This behavior doesn't just affect your relationship—it stunts your personal growth.

"Alcohol brings out the parts of you both that you have not worked on."

Overworking can also be a significant sabotage factor. Many men get frustrated with the energy at home and throw themselves into work. Putting your energy into work seems like an effective short-term solution, but ultimately, it leads to loneliness and a disconnect from your wife, making your home life even more strained.

A: Approval and Accountability

Are you constantly trying to prove you're a great man? This need often originates from a long-standing desire for validation and approval written deep within your programming. This quest to prove your worth can trap you in a cycle where you always try to avoid disapproval and failure. This pressure creates a distorted reality where you overemphasize your successes and minimize your failures, causing you to drive your wife away by trying to convince her, over and over, that you are a good man.

This behavior often leads to self-victimization, where you blame your wife for not recognizing your efforts. It's a vicious cycle that keeps you from genuinely engaging with her and running in circles, trying to prove something that ultimately doesn't lead to true fulfillment or happiness. Instead of controlling your emotions, you blame her for your failures as you run yourself off the track.

If you need to prove yourself—explanation or defensiveness—it's because you lack confidence and integrity. You need to hold yourself accountable. Or she will. You can begin your real work when you let this sink in.

F: Fight, Flight, Freeze, or Fawn

Our responses to threat-based situations are complex. My default was fight mode, but I sometimes shifted to flight mode as I locked myself away with alcohol to avoid dealing with problems directly. This avoidance, while peaceful now, prevented genuine resolution and growth. It's also a prime example of how coping mechanisms impede connection.

In fight mode, aggressive confrontations escalate quickly and cause the kind of damage people tell you is irreparable. Flight mode reveals our lack of commitment facing hard conversations because we avoid them, resulting in deeper disconnection. Freezing occurs when you're overwhelmed and unsure how to proceed, reminding your wife that she has to mother you. Fawning involves excessive placating, trying desperately to keep the peace by any means necessary, often at the cost of your integrity.

E: Enforcing Boundaries

You try to enforce boundaries you probably will need to follow through on. Are you even in a position to effectively implement them?

Within my program, I advocate that setting boundaries should be a last resort, not the natural reaction the world pushes. Boundaries should not be used lightly; they are fundamentally about protecting yourself, not controlling or punishing others. That means you can have zero contempt attached to them.

"Then it makes no sense to 'lay' a boundary when the world tells you to use one."

Worse, if you're laying boundaries when your wife doesn't respect you, it's unlikely she'll respect your boundaries either. Boundaries truly work only when you embody the integrity and respect of the 'new' man. Many men set boundaries from a place of desperation, like saying, "If you cheat on me again, it's over," or "You can't speak to me that way, or I'll leave." These are reactions to a heightened level of disrespect that has been allowed to escalate over time. When boundaries stem from this place, your wife sees them as empty threats from a desperate man.

Consider the progression of disconnection in your relationship. It may have started with passive-aggressive remarks, led to belittling, and eventually evolved into outright contemptuous behavior: throwing things, kicking you in the balls, cheating. By the time you're setting a boundary, it's often a reaction to the build-up of these issues—situations where you feel powerless and are grasping at control.

When you fail to enforce these 'ultimatums,' you appear weak or stupid. Previous discussions on maintaining credibility and respect in relationships have revealed the ineffectiveness of boundaries. Setting a boundary in these circumstances often involves reacting to protect yourself from further hurt rather than proactively providing a future-paced structure.

"Everything you do should be structured for your goals in the future."

Instead of laying down ultimatums, you can provide a constructive approach of leading by example and getting ahead of problems before they escalate to severe levels. The same approach works for your past issues. This involves understanding and addressing those underlying issues in your relationship.

For example, disconnection or lack of mutual respect are explored in depth throughout the book. By focusing on positive engagement and creating a respectful and supportive environment, you can preempt the need for rigid boundaries and cultivate a relationship based on mutual respect and understanding.

"Inspire while you are learning the skills. Lead her as you use them. Ask her to join you if you need to. Only if you must, MOTIVATE her with boundaries."

To truly move your marriage forward and regain a position of influence (in front of the pace car), it's critical to respond thoughtfully rather than react defensively. Shift from SAFE Reactions—where you protect yourself from perceived threats—to STAT Responses and build safety and trust, strengthening the connection with your wife.

"With STAT, you inspire and lead by moving her past the issues and staying out in front of new issues rather than scrambling to contain them."

STATRESPONSE

Structure: Am I providing structure or direction for where we want to go?

T

Triggers: Am I, or are both of us, being triggered? {Love her through it}

A

Am I, or can I provide Adventure: Did I or could I provide drama, intrigue and escape to create positive emotional tension? Curiosity?

T

Tests: Am I being tested? Is it subconscious or conscious?

STAT Response:

I am renowned for transforming marriages by teaching men how to elevate themselves. It's crucial to understand that while the initial focus will be on you and your end goal is reconnecting with your wife, the principles laid out in this book apply universally across all your relationships. Whether you're separated, divorced, or dealing with a particularly challenging relationship with your wife—a "vicious Type 3," as we've discussed—you must begin applying STAT Responses in all interactions, not just with your wife.

We're shifting from SAFE Reactions to STAT Responses. This change is foundational for men who aspire to lead in their relationships effectively. Consider how this applies not just to your wife but also to interactions with your children. Every man desires admiration and respect from his family—to be built up by his wife and revered in front of others.

Let's paint this picture to understand this concept better: Imagine you're at a party, surrounded by people, with your wife proudly by your side. She engages in conversation in such a way that highlights your best qualities, demonstrating her admiration and respect for you. This is the image of a powerful, loving partnership that you want—one where your wife is deeply connected to you, not distracted or distant.

If your wife is cold or dismissive, it's a sign that she doesn't feel safe or respected. To change this, you must consistently demonstrate the qualities of the new man you've become rather than falling back into old patterns. Your responses must show you're a Man with Impact—this will solidify the respect and admiration of your wife and children.

Understanding and mastering STAT Responses is challenging but crucial. This chapter will provide further lessons and tools to not only learn STAT but embody it. Remember, even if you feel you've mastered these skills, it's easy to lose your footing and blame your wife for derailing your progress.

I'll equip you with practical STAT Responses for everyday situations to help keep you on course. Additionally, other resources like my anxiety training—which I personally use—will support you in maintaining a responsive stance in stressful situations.

These strategies revolve around "I" statements, focusing on what you can control and improve, regardless of how your wife may be SAFE Reacting. No matter how difficult you think your situation is, consistently providing a safe, respectful environment will create the trust and respect that allows your wife to feel secure and valued.

"The respect is earned in the disrespect."

Given the complexities of learning and implementing STAT Responses, I strongly recommend joining our specialized training in Lords, where you'll find extensive resources, role-playing opportunities, and community support to enhance your skills. For more information and to engage directly with these tools, visit https://MorrowMarriage.com/tools. This step is essential for anyone serious about making lasting changes in their relationships.

S.T.A.T.

S: is for Structure
T: is for Triggers
A: is for Adventure
T: is for Tests

S: Structure

Am I providing structure for the direction I want this to go? Leading at home does not mean using manipulative or controlling behavior. Authentic leadership is about creating a partnership where both individuals can thrive. Take Kathryn, a powerhouse recognized by Forbes, Entrepreneur Magazine, and more. As a leading voice for women globally through her work with The White Picket Fence Project, her achievements highlight her strength, and my leadership at home does not diminish her capabilities; they complement them.

"When you lead correctly, each of your strengths will lift the other's weaknesses."

Society bombards us with mixed messages from social media and contentious movements like feminism and #MeToo, and it's easy to get lost in debates about masculinity. These discussions often polarize opinions, leading to extremes of "toxic" or "alpha" masculinity. It's time to cut through the noise. Your role isn't about adhering to these labels but about becoming the leader in your relationship, guiding you and your wife to become what I like to call a "Superpower Couple."

"Forget #CoupleGoals"

For most men, reality hardly reflects the dynamics of a Superpower Couple. Typically, the wife organizes the calendar and makes all the decisions for everything and everyone in the home. This includes daily routines, all aspects of their shared lives, and even the dynamics of communication and intimacy. This dynamic can leave men feeling sidelined in their relationships, where they begin to think they're neglected or unimportant.

To shift this paradigm, you must start by establishing yourself as a partner who can transition into a leadership role. This means providing structure and direction, regardless of any resistance from your wife. You must envision the "Future us" and start acting in ways that align with that vision.

What would you and your wife be doing right now if you were already the couple you aspire to be? That's the mindset you need to adopt. Provide structure by doing what this "Future Us" would do in this vision, and do not get input from your wife about if she's not on board yet. You'll see how this comes together as you progress.

"Do what future you would do—future you will thank you."

This does not mean imposing your will but guiding the marriage towards shared goals and values, new and old. In the upcoming chapters, we'll dive deeper into how you can effectively lead and create this collaborative dynamic. It starts with you setting the tone and pace, demonstrating through actions—not just words—how you envision your future. This is the essence of providing structure in a relationship that honors and elevates you and your wife. When we discuss purpose and impact, you will find this also applies to people in life.

T: Triggers

Am I empathizing when she's triggered? Pay attention here. As a man, you are a protector. This has been a reality from the dawn of time. This role extends into managing emotional situations effectively. You must be there for your wife before you need to feel or share your emotions openly.

Emotional safety is as important as physical safety. It's crucial to acknowledge that while emotions are often viewed as more feminine, having emotions is human, and managing them is essential. You must handle your feelings without overwhelming your wife, especially when she is triggered. In other words, you cannot puke your feelings all over your wife while attempting to get your own needs met.

"This is especially important if you are in the middle of 'understanding' your wife."

Remember, the triggers your wife experiences may have been present before you met her, and you may have inadvertently stacked them. Understand that any 'red flags' you see in your marriage are likely ones you've helped create and raise. The priority is to address her triggers by providing a safe space where she can express her feelings without fear. This involves responding to her pain first and ensuring she feels seen, heard, and understood.

A friend of mine, Travis Neville, author of *Reviving Masculinity*, describes a trigger and response well. Noting that the trigger is the stimulus: "As a man, we live in the gap between stimulus and response. Master that space." In other words, you are accountable for that space between the trigger and your response. To take my STAT Response further, I would add:

"You can help her put the gun down."

You should note that most men can quickly get stuck in a happy wife, happy life, validation, and placating phase when using STAT. That is not the point. STAT begins with structure for the future and does not end with your validating or empathizing with her trigger. Always remember to future-pace when responding with STAT.

A: Adventure

If nearly every man spends too much time on triggers when focused on STAT, what should they do instead? Adventure is where it's at. When thinking about the structure of where you want to go, you use adventure to take you there. I cannot stress this enough: STAT Response is likely the hardest thing you must learn once you've exited the Nice Guy Triangle. More on that later.

"Do not fall into happy wife, happy life (in the triggers) and pump yourself up believing you're using STAT."

Am I bringing adventure into our relationship? Adventure is essential—not just in the form of physical activities but as a means to introduce positive emotional tension that counteracts daily life's mundane or stressful aspects. It's indispensable in a negative situation. Women, just like men, are drawn towards drama. Most women, though, crave drama, intrigue, and escape. This need for emotional stimulation is why we often turn to television, books, social media, or hobbies. Curiosity and fun are your two most essential tools when providing adventure.

"Curiosity did not kill the cat. Comfort and complacency made you a pussy, and lions have more fun."

If your wife is bringing drama into the relationship, it's a sign she may be seeking more positive emotional tension. The Magnet in Man at Play will flip negative emotional tension (drama) into positive emotional tension (intrigue). The Player makes it more fun. Using adventure to elevate her mood or distract her from stressors like a tough day at work or even jealousy can be incredibly effective. It's about proactively creating engaging and exciting experiences that enrich your relationship.

When you realize you can provide all the positive feelings she needs to move forward, you can rise out of the past. Men tend to be hyper-focused on their negative emotions and miss opportunities to create positive emotions and the connection that results from their wives. This is another example of your wife leading you. Instead, show her what she's missing with adventure.

T: Tests

Am I being tested? It's easy to mistake an accountability tests, especially in relationships. A test is often a natural reaction to your integrity and reliability and is related to accountability. Tests are not exclusive to women, but women get a bad rap for this. For example, if you've repeatedly failed to meet your New Year's resolutions, even your friends will take your commitments with a grain of salt.

Your wife's reminders about household chores aren't always tests but call for accountability based on experiences. She needs to know she can rely on you and that you can manage your responsibilities and her emotions without collapsing under pressure. Consistent reliability builds trust and respect.

As you will soon see from some examples below, your ability to hold structure and provide adventure, no matter her emotions, proves your reliability. This consistency is crucial for leadership. Without it, you're merely reacting to her cues rather than setting the pace for the race. Passing these tests is how you'll get in front of the pace car and make your laps to the checkered flag.

In cases of conscious testing, understand that it's not manipulation but an evaluation of security. If your wife challenges you, it's often because she needs assurance that she can depend on you—that you can lead her—even when she pushes you. Women value safety as a top priority. Many men think she's trying to run them off the track when she wants you to take the lead!

Reliability, integrity, and consistency are key to passing these tests. Remember, as the man in the relationship you are meant to be the rock, the lighthouse, the shoreline, and the shoulder to cry on. Embodying these roles is rare but essential for building a robust and enduring marriage. Unfortunately, this man barely exists in the world today. Wives are waiting.

Love Her Through It:

Before we go further, let's discuss effective ways to establish a safe place for your wife to feel - and share those feelings without fear of your reactions. This foundation allows her to be unapologetically herself; she opens up to you with a deeper level of emotional connection between you both.

Validation plays a critical role in nurturing this connection. When your wife is emotionally triggered, remember that it's not your role to "fix" the issue as you perceive it. As a masculine presence, your job is to provide space for her to experience and process her emotions without fear of judgment or criticism. Most often, she's seeking empathy, not solutions or lectures.

It's important to note that validation doesn't mean agreement. Your wife may express feelings that you think are irrational, unfounded, or wrong. The goal here is to create a space where her feminine energy can freely express and work through these emotions. If you need help understanding her perspective, approach it with curiosity rather than skepticism.

Asking, "Could you tell me more about that?" shows that you're genuinely interested in understanding her feelings. Responses like "I appreciate where you are coming from" or "That sucks" are far more supportive than any lecture that dismisses her feelings and damages your connection.

As you work on breaking down the walls built up over time, you will get covered in dust and likely get hit on the head with a few bricks. It may seem like things are getting worse when your wife begins to express her emotions freely—this is a positive development.

She might puke her feelings more than before, but this gives you a prime opportunity to demonstrate your growth in handling emotions effectively without resorting to old patterns. I've found this challenging myself as someone who struggled with narcissism and a complete lack of empathy. The most successful men, and their incredible testimonials, come from coaching during this transition. As it helps guide them in recognizing and processing emotions more adeptly and with more rapid results. Empathy is a struggle for me; however, if I can relate what Kathryn is feeling to a time I felt that same feeling, I can fall into a more empathetic state.

"The stronger your emotional connection becomes and the more empathetic your wife is with you again, the better you will empathize."

This approach lays the groundwork for peace within your home. By responding with empathy, curiosity, and genuine validation, you'll show your wife how much you value and appreciate her. She needs to feel seen and heard, not lectured or misunderstood. She will feel more connected to you once she realizes that you're truly listening and not trying to correct her emotions. The old days of talking at her—talking your way into your head, heart, or vagina—will be behind you once you master STAT Responses.

Let's use practical examples of applying STAT Responses in common scenarios you might face. These examples will help illustrate how you can validate her feelings and opinions without necessarily agreeing with them and move her into the future. Your mission is to appreciate your wife regardless of your opinion. When you can handle her explosive emotions and respond accordingly, she begins to trust you, and you will be well on your way to reinforcing the Peace Pillar in your home.

"Sometimes, you will be the crash test dummy and drive into the wall yourself."

STAT in Action:

Last Thanksgiving, Kathryn was upset I was cleaning the garage instead of loading the turkey in the oven. Frustrated, she said, "Where were you?? The turkey needed to go in the oven. I did it myself." I responded with STAT:

"Oh, you're right. That must be frustrating for you, Baby Cakes." I paused, let her frustration deflate for a moment, and then picked her up and said, "If you wanted to see my muscles in action, you just had to say so." I smiled, squeezed her biceps, and said, "We are a hot couple." Then, in a disappointed, gentle tone, I said, "Lucky turkey."

When you master this, you will future-pace everything with negative tension. While you're busy defending yourself, proving you're awesome for cleaning the garage, or busy apologizing for something you don't need to be sorry for, I validated Kathryn's emotions, reminded her that holidays are more fun with humor than frustration, reminded her that we are a Superpower Couple and flirted—without puking any of that.

You will use STAT for the rest of your life, but it won't always be over tough issues. Your wife just wants to feel safe enough to express her emotions. When she does, you will deepen your connection more each day. I cannot express how much gratitude and respect I have earned from Kathryn since creating STAT.

"And I love the connecting, too."

When your wife's scrolling on the phone:

Structure:

She's annoyed. She may come at you with a sharp "I'm on the phone," or maybe she's polite: "I just need a minute, Babe." It doesn't matter where she's at. You need to provide structure. For starters, put your phone away. If you have to, you keep it off, upside down, or in another room.

Triggers:

We want to love her through it, but we have not determined the problem. For some of you, she might be bored and scrolling. Kathryn loves her dog rescue, animal-infested newsfeed. I used to jump the gun with thoughts of a potential emotional affair or worse. Maybe you've already begun to let insecurity grip you.

She must be talking with the guy. Who is he? Many of you will have a wife who doesn't want to talk to you. For most, that's the trigger. As you'll see in the Rejection Ladder, talking leads to banter and fun. Fun leads you to connection. Connection leads to dating and flirting. Flirting leads to sex. She's not interested in that yet, so she's spending quality time with her phone.

Since we know it could be as simple as her not wanting to let things go further than a conversation, don't assume anything here. Do not let insecurity take over. Put your phone away, provide structure, and say, "Hey, Babe, I get that. I'm about to..." Fill in the blank with the adventure you're about to have. Maybe you grab her hand. You turn the music on and start dancing. She'll probably shut you down if that's where you two are. Don't take it personally.

Adventure:

Dance by yourself. Another option, as you'll learn later in Man with Purpose, is to create polarity, becoming the Magnet by using your purposes and truly being unaffected by her rejections. In that case, you would move on with your day.

Test:

The test here is handling her rejections confidently. You cannot let your insecurities take over. As soon as you feel your anxiety creep in, remember that you are creating an opportunity to connect. Your job is simple. You cannot sit there, too available for your wife and desperately waiting. Remember, when your wife is on a pedestal, she's looking down on you. When you are a valuable dude, you're unaffected. You've got a lot on the go, and she just missed out.

When your wife rejects your flirts:

Your wife is bending over in the fridge, and her butt is up in the air. Most of us, ass-man or not, love our wife's ass. I sure love Kathryn's. Do what I do. Say, "Ooh Baby... way at the back. Waaaaay at the back." Kathryn will shake her bum in the air for me and flirt back. That can go wherever it goes. But it wasn't always like that. She often would have been annoyed or flirted back because she felt she had to fake it. Many of you will have wives who turn around and roll their eyes at you.

Some wives don't want any of it and are rude. "Stop it, you idiot. You're not gettin' any of this." Or, right to it, "All you think about is sex." Some wives can get quite mean, especially around sex. No problem. This is one of the most straightforward STAT Responses ever. Provide structure, love her through it, provide adventure, and pass her test all at once.

Structure/Triggers/Adventure/Test:

Reply simply, "I married you, and I got that! BOOM!" Then, move in the direction that you are already going. Were you going to the bathroom? Making a sandwich? Heading to the office for your book or the garage to leave somewhere? I don't really care. Jump right into whatever you're doing because you care about a lot more than sex. It's not about her accepting or reciprocating your flirtation. You love your wife, she's got a hot ass, and you let her know. But you're a valuable dude, and you have shit to do. Go do it.

When your wife won't engage or go on dates with you:

In Man at Play, we will cover seven types of dates. For now, I want to run through a standard rejection whether you're roommates, she's coasting, or you're enemies. Let's say you set up a date, any type, and your wife says, "No, I'm not going," she's rude or ignores you. It doesn't matter if she's polite or impolite, just like her rejection at the fridge. We will do a simple STAT Response here, and these opportunities show her what she's missing.

Structure:

You go on the date. I know it's scary, but there's your structure.

Triggers:

The trigger we need to love her through will be based on what she says. Remember, no matter what, this will make no sense to her. Suppose the trigger is wrapped up in everything you do without her. In that case, she has not felt like a priority to you. You'll hear something like, "You're so selfish" because you're going anyway. Since you're not trying to go without her, you will validate her feelings even though you disagree. "I have been pretty shitty with prioritizing you, haven't I?" Then go back to the structure and say, "Throw on that pink dress. We'll leave in 20."

Adventure/Test:

You set a tone for marriage and leadership by breaking your need to follow her lead. Whether she's rejecting you or she's tired and canceling, you go. Of course, this is different the closer you are to the "New" Marriage you're creating. For now, you go without her. You're passing her test, but it will not feel like it.

You want to be with your wife. However, you are showing your wife that you can survive without her, and there's a lot more life where you are going. She is missing out.

For a bonus adventure, throw in a little reminder while you're out and when you come home. Order a plate of food for her at the restaurant and take a selfie with her empty chair and her plate, captioned with, "Well, this is awkward." Don't forget to bring her food home to her! While you're out, have a blast. It may seem counterintuitive, but remember, you are providing structure. What do you have to do if you want to have fun on hot dates? Go on dates.

When you know or find out your wife is cheating:

This is one of the toughest situation to be in. If you're going through this, I am sorry for your pain. But you are not going to sit and play in it. You are going to move forward. Like all disrespect, the man you were before led here. It is natural to embrace SAFE Reactions. Your self-worth has been attacked in the worst way. Your urge to defend yourself, lecture on all the reasons you are good enough, and blame her for failing as a wife is overwhelming.

This disrespect didn't happen overnight. Dig deep and own what caused her to not look to you. Why did she need to look elsewhere for safety and connection? There is power in overcoming the failures that pushed her away, and the impact that comes with embracing your growth is the only path toward pulling her out of the affair.

Structure:

To be clear, I do not condone cheating. However, you will not speak about the affair, bring it up, lecture her on the rules of marriage, look at her phone, go through her computer, track her location, or pick through the garbage looking for condoms. That is all playing in your pain and chasing insecurity. Everything listed will only make the affair feel safer than you. The affair can be addressed at some point if needed. Today, you don't have the skills or respect necessary for it to be effective.

"Focus on your growth, level up, and present the best, most authentic version of yourself."

Triggers:

At a minimum, your insecurities triggered this. Your interrogations and lectures pushed her away long before she made these terrible mistakes. She justifies what she is doing by focusing on your past behavior. Be careful validating these feelings. Focus more on defeating the triggers with adventure. This situation is incredibly sensitive and very specific for men and their stories. I recommend catered advice with Lord's coaching calls. You will have to walk a fine line and risk triggering guilty feelings. No positive feelings will come from her negative emotions, especially if you trigger more.

Adventure:

Create a safe container for her to feel, and she will see you. She will observe the Insecurity Monster not taking over. The Anger Beast is restrained. That shift in behavior is likely to spark some level of curiosity. Keep building on that safety. If she goes out, smile and ask if she had a good time when you welcome her home. Later, she'll reflect, trying to figure out what she's missing.

She may be having an emotional affair on her phone. Grab her attention with a funny meme or send a selfie. You will not spam her with messages or pictures but keep the bids for connection flowing.

"Your goal is to be busy as a Man with Kids, a Man with Purpose, using Morrow Momentum and a possible partnership with me and the Lords. More on this later."

Test:

The real test is providing a safe environment as a Man with Impact as long as possible. Eventually, she will feel open enough to tell you about the affair, in which case you'll run through the STAT. Can you use curiosity while keeping the monster at bay? "Oh my gosh, I...I... understand why you felt that way. Like... no wonder you had to... you know, find somewhere else to go." It's okay to stutter like this. It's painful. It would be unnatural to confidently speak here, no matter how much you have released your wife.

Love her through it.

Do not rush the adventure here. We can turn this into a more exciting and fun adventure when the time is right. The idea is to let her feel. That's what impact is all about: get her feelings out. Once she knows it's safe to have those feelings, she can embrace them (and you), becoming more emotionally connected to you again.

Start letting everything else go and allowing your intimacy to build. When she's in a safe enough place to tell you about it, you don't come unglued, insecurity doesn't rule you, and anger doesn't destroy everything—at that moment, the affair will begin to lose its appeal. We all do it wrong until we learn…

"Most men in the world are not leveling up. You are a Lord rising. You will come out on top."

When you initiate sex, but your wife rejects you:

This is one of the easiest times for us to get your wife to run into the side of your car because you're a man; you have needs. We'll cover a lot of this in Man in Control. Still, when you realize that you've been using SAFE reactions to destroy the intimacy in your marriage, you also realize exactly how much you can contribute to its salvation. You will stop pouting or getting frustrated and angry. You'll stop the "talks" with your wife about it. You won't be watching porn. These SAFE reactions are all part of how you have wasted time and energy away from solving the problem and made it worse.

Structure:

Timing is a common issue for couples, especially when you have kids. I'm going to use two examples. I recall a man from my program. He had the kids all lined up with iPads. His wife was busy cleaning their bedroom. He went in, closed the door, locked it, made his move, and she rejected him. He was upset. Extremely upset.

Another typical example for men is when you have your whole day and night but wait until you go to bed. You make your move right when your wife's already falling asleep. She shoots you down, but what do you do? Many of you pout your way out of the bedroom, flip on some porn, and jerk off. Don't you think she notices?

The fastest way to kill your wife's libido is to make her think you are a big, whiny toddler who acts out. In both these cases, this is terrible timing. We'll talk about sex later in the program; however, in these examples, you have already screwed up with a lack of structure. We can't do much about poor timing when it's too late.

Triggers:

You won't focus on triggers here or loving her through it in the moment. You're going to love her through it differently. Consider the longer-term, loving her through it and giving her peace and safety. Later, in Man in Control, we'll work on your expectations. This will relieve a lot of the pressure she feels. She will begin to think that your expectations have changed. Pressure is relieved as time passes. You won't invoke curiosity immediately but can provide adventure and pass the test.

Adventure:

Let's turn it around and have some fun. So, she rejects you. It doesn't matter if she rejects you lovingly, like, "No, Babe, I love you. I'm exhausted. I hope you sleep well". Or if she's insulting, "You're so gross. Ugh, get off me." You handle it the same way. I always like to provide a little adventure and have a little fun with it because wives want to sleep with fun guys.

Girls like to have fun. It's no secret. With a smile, all you need to do is respond: "I was hoping you'd say no, Babe. I'm hornier on Wednesdays." Read the room and adjust the specific day of the week to your situation. The point is to have fun with it.

"Girls Just Wanna Have Fun, by Cindy Lauper. The song's still popular today for a reason."

Several of you have a Pavlovian response to giving your wife a hug, kiss, or a massage. Unfortunately, you've conditioned her to dread the otherwise pleasant activity. Imagine you're on the couch, and she's enthralled in a book. You make a move, and she rejects you. You're interrupting her reading time. You're ready to storm off with your phone, already frantically tapping to find your go-to coping mechanism. Why not turn the tables with some fun? You make your move, and you can say something like, "Ah! You perv! I'm just gonna give you a rub. Give me your legs". Grab a leg, and you start massaging. You can do anything to keep the momentum going in a fun, adventurous way.

Test:

This test is passed as you adopt a mindset that consistently brings positive energy to every aspect of your life. Once you flip that switch, everything falls into place more quickly. The polarity you generate draws her closer to you, as your wife notices her rejections no longer affect you negatively. You naturally respond playfully, and your wins begin stacking up. In a second rejection, you STAT again.

"You'll be flipping rejections to invitations in no time."

When your wife wants a separation or divorce:

Often, men follow me because they feel blindsided by their wife's sudden demand for separation or divorce. It's a shock that, despite the warning signs you understand from reading this book, we rarely see this coming. Whether your wife wants separate bedrooms or separation from the home, requests or demands a divorce, or serves you papers, we will handle this all the same way.

"I was handed divorce papers with eight weeks to go before they were finalized and that's when I found Cass. Five weeks later, she said "Do what you want with them." so I ripped them up." — William (Bill) Glenn: Mentor to Lords.

You need to provide structure to move the marriage in the direction you want. Your wife is checked out now. She's leading you. Get out in front of the pace car first by not caving to her demands. You will decide this is where you're going, and you're not working on this apart.

Structure:

When she says you must leave the bedroom, you won't sleep on the couch. If she says I want you to leave this house right now, you do not leave. Next, she will give you all kinds of reasons why you need to leave. Leaving is a step toward separation. Separation is a step toward divorce. Do not move in a direction you do not want the relationship to go. You must maintain your impact, providing the structure for where you're taking the marriage.

Triggers:

When she starts telling you why this won't work, you're changing for her; she doesn't believe you, it's too little, too late, etcetera, you'll love her through every single one of them. You are one big, giant trigger for her, so she's trying to separate or get divorced. Just appreciate what she says. You're reading this book, which means you get it.

Even if some of what she says is untrue, it doesn't matter. You were already taking responsibility after reaching some form of rock bottom. Be prepared to demonstrate your understanding with "Yeah, Babe, I can understand why you'd say that." or "Oh wow. That would be hard. It makes sense why you're done." As long as you understand your wife, you keep rolling through the validation. When she starts to ask you questions, you'll answer them. She might ask, "Why do you even want to stay here?" Your answer would be something like: "I love you. And I'm starting to realize how much I've really screwed up." Let her get freaking mad. Let her feel. Let her explode. This is what we want. I know it's hard. You want to protect yourself with a SAFE Reaction. Remember what you're trying to do here as a Man with Impact.

Adventure:

You may or may not have some options for Adventure. For example, you might throw in, "Because I fucking love you." Then squeeze her face or pick her up and twirl her. Let her get mad. Men get validation all wrong. You need to understand that when your wife is done, she's saying and doing things that don't add up. If you want her, don't defend yourself. Understand her and protect your future. You are validating her and providing some love and fun to change the tone. Please don't go into detail about the new you, me, or the book. No SAFE Reacting. Just have some fun while showing her what the future looks like. No matter how bleak it seems in moments like this.

Test:

If you can keep showing up using this book and the program, being a Lord and not the man you were, she will see the different behaviors, actions, and responses —the New Man. You are going to have so many opportunities. For example, most of you have kids. We can use kids to show up as the New Man. Not just with your kids but because you have kids. You will still be connecting over or talking about them. You are learning how to create opportunities as we work through this book.

"Just do everything I say, I'm serious. Everything."

STAT Responses and Kathryn's Half Rap (coming up later in Man with Impact) are the most challenging things to teach through writing. You don't see my body language. You don't hear my tone. You don't notice my facial expressions or pauses between words or sentences. You cannot hear the empathy. I encourage you to practice your STAT responses using someone in your life you trust or join Lords and take advantage of coaching or live STAT training at https://MorrowMarriage.com/Tools.

Use Man with Impact and STAT Responses, and then we'll start to learn the rest of the system. Listen, when your wife is done, it's scary. I get it. Soon, you'll be showing up as a 10, and your wife must meet you. The dating pool sucks out there.

"Her bucket list never included a separation, divorce, or seeing her kids 50 percent of the time."

You have so much more going for you. So, let go of the SAFE Reactions and focus on STAT Responses.

Your First STAT Response:

Engaging with your work—referencing me, exploring my social media, diving into The Reset, and continuing your personal growth—is essential. Let me guide you through a proactive STAT Response, setting you up to overcome potential challenges and potentially making things much smoother.

When your wife discovers my program—perhaps through my book, our podcast, my app, or other channels—she may react negatively and strongly for several reasons:

1. Mad Passion and Glorious Sex Life: Describing the 'New' Marriage, I often express my thoughts on passion and intimacy. If your wife seems disinterested, either with you or in general, she'll feel offended.

2. Personal Change: Your wife might already believe you won't change, or changes won't last because she thinks you're changing for her. She may also be feeling it's too little, too late. In this case, she'll potentially be angry with you.

3. Emotional Distance: Some wives may feel so disconnected—to the point of considering infidelity or even divorce, driven by a lack of fulfillment or unresolved issues. She may feel guilty or ashamed of her choices and blame you for sharing too many personal details.

4. Financial Skepticism: If there's a lack of trust, even a $30 book might seem like a waste of money and time. She might view the time spent on calls or engaging with my program as wasteful.

5. Pure Terror or the "Ick": She may find out how abusive I was to Kathryn or that I am a managing narcissist. This can be initially off-putting until she realizes that if I could change, so can you.

"There are far too many reasons for me to explain each of these points. However, when you begin to struggle, if you're not using Morrow Momentum, realize that's the exact reason you're struggling."

The following section, "Your Comfort Zone," includes a homework assignment to prepare you for your first significant conversation. This exercise will help you address and clear the air about these sensitive issues. Removing the elephant in the room and responding thoughtfully will pave the way for more open and effective conversations with your wife.

"I've become so good at STAT; my wife and I just had the most equal conversation we've ever had." —Matty Sterlo, AU: Mentor to Lords.

Your Comfort Zone Part I:

In this book, I'll push you to stretch your boundaries, often far beyond your comfort zone. Whether you realize it yet or not, there's an underlying fear in your relationship with your wife. For some, it's about how she reacts; for others, it's the fear of losing her. Many of you want to be wanted again, which forces you to hide your true self.

The first step is to embrace that fear. You wouldn't be reading this if you weren't seeking more from your marriage and perhaps from life itself. By the end of this journey, you'll discover true freedom, and your wife will be right there with you. Realize this: without your wife and your current failures, you wouldn't be motivated to rise, grow, and become the Lord—the man, husband, father, and leader in life—you were born to be.

Do not feel ashamed of pursuing personal growth. Despite any past failings in your relationship, you are committed to this path, which will transform you. Here's your first task: put this book down, open your phone's camera app, and record a short video. Smile and say:

"Baby!... I just want to say thank you... I've been reflecting and doing a terrible job of owning up to who I am... Who I've been...I love you."

This is not about announcing your new journey but expressing gratitude, acknowledging you are taking responsibility, and breaking through your initial fear without sharing any explanation. Send her the video.

Her response might vary—she may engage with questions or ignore them. If she ignores it, consider your part done for now, though she may bring it up later. When she does respond, stick to STAT. Remember, like everyone else:

"She doesn't give a shit who you're going to be, only who you are, and that's defined by how you've made her feel in the past."

Structure:

Ensure you're not just trying to win her with words or prove your worth. If she asks why you sent the video, keep it simple—you should sound excited: "Oh! I've been following this guy on social media. I've realized I need to take much more responsibility for the kind of man and husband I've been. Who knew?"

Triggers:

If this is the first time she's visibly upset, remember, it's not about defending yourself or retaliating. You're acknowledging your role in past issues.

Adventure:

Be enthusiastic. Speak slowly, clearly, and pause thoughtfully. Address her queries, but hold off on apologizing—you might not fully understand what you need to apologize for. If appropriate, you might say, "I'm sorry for blaming you for our problems and not taking responsibility." Then, add, "I'm just starting to see things clearly. I just wanted to start by thanking you. I love you." Express excitement about the future, "I'll have more to share soon. For now, I need to get to work." Give her a moment more of your presence before moving on.

Curiosity:

If she's curious about the book or my program, invite her to explore further. You could say, "Would you like to know more?" and direct her to my social media or our podcast, 'Morrow Marriage,' where my wife Kathryn and I discuss our experiences and insights. You still need to get to work. Go back to the adventure.

Test:

This is a critical moment, and the only way to navigate it successfully is by adhering to the principles laid out in this book. Importantly, do not suggest she join Kathryn in The White Picket Fence Project. This stage of your journey is about you taking responsibility, as a program like Kathryn's or suggesting couples therapy might make her feel cornered.

"You cannot simultaneously take responsibility and blame your wife. Suggesting she gets to work is as though you are blaming her."

REJECTIONLADDER
IS SHE DOING A JOB? IS IT OUT OF PITY OR FEAR?
DOES SHE INITIATE? DESIRE TO DESIRE OR AT LEAST, DESIRE TO CONNECT?
SEX
WHAT'S THE TEASING LIKE? MASCULINE TOUCH?
ARE YOU LEAVING CLUES FOR WHERE TOUCH WILL GO?
FLIRTING-SEXUAL
WHAT ARE YOUR DATES LIKE? SAME OLD OR HAVING A BLAST?
DATES
WHAT'S THE BANTER LIKE? AFFIRMATIONS, GRATITUDE? SUPPORTIVE TOUCH?
FLIRTING NON-SEXUAL
ARE YOU JUMPING TOPIC TO TOPIC? ARE YOU LAUGHING? HAVING FUN?
CONVERSATION
WHAT'S YOUR ENERGY LIKE?
ENERGY
SWEEP UP THE EGGSHEELS

Rejection Ladder Part I:

Understanding rejection is key to navigating your relationship. It's common to revert to our standard SAFE Reactions when we feel rejected, but this does little to change the pattern of ongoing rejections. It's crucial to honestly assess your current position on the Rejection Ladder, where each rung represents a level of intimate connection with your wife that you should aspire to achieve.

Many men either focus too early on the higher rungs or neglect the foundational ones as they progress. To create intimacy, you must reinforce each rung as you ascend. This will reduce the impact of inevitable rejection and keep you from sliding back down. Progressing up the ladder starts with simple connections that will eventually build toward deep emotional and physical connections.

"I can't believe any leading man before me did not create something like this. You're welcome."

The Base:

Start at the base. You won't stay here long but you can't skip over any rung as you climb. This is a shift away from insecurity, anxiety, and fear. It's a place where you sweep up the eggshells. Imagine how you would feel if your wife was about to jump you as you walked through the door. You'd feel confident. You would feel alive. And I'm sure you'd be present. These qualities would make you a safe space or refuge where your wife could express herself. Your mood would be constant, especially at home, no longer dictated by the day's stress and, better yet, by your wife's and kids' emotions.

The 1st Rung:

The goal of his rung is to maintain your positive energy regardless of how your wife reacts. You set the emotional tempo by engaging in light everyday conversations like, "How was your day?" or sharing stories like, "You should have seen Riddick today! He loves playing with his swords!" These interactions show that you are invested in your wife, the atmosphere of your home, and your family.

The 2nd Rung:

Stepping up on the ladder turns these small interactions into meaningful conversations. She may test you, and as you pass these tests, deeper discussions become easier and pave the way toward intimacy. You may feel awkward, but remember your role in rising up the ladder. Never forget to bring this mindset about conversation to interactions with your kids. Be curious about your wife and remember this rung when you add in #morrowmomentum later.

The 3rd Rung:

Engage in non-sexual flirting, touching, affirmations, and expressions of gratitude. Use your wit for good. While more physical touch will be covered in Man at Play, begin with simple hugs, hello-and-goodbye kisses, sitting close on the couch, or a reassuring hand on her back when you express love.

The 4th Rung:

What do your dates look like? There are seven types of dates we'll explore in Man at Play. For now, consider any activity you can do at home or away as an opportunity for a fun date. Engage in lively conversations that skip from one topic to another. Focus on laughing, dreaming, and truly enjoying each other.

The 5th Rung:

Elevate to sexual flirting. By now you have shifted the tone at home and, by using STAT, artfully handle rejections, making her feel comfortable in your presence. It's time to increase your playful banter, make flirting more direct and intimate, setting the stage for the good stuff. We'll dive deep into tis in Man at Play.

The 6th Rung:

You've reached the peak, the top rung! Here, the concept of 'Job Sex' is a thing of the past. Both of you feel deeply connected and ready to fully embrace this stage. Man in Control will detail the seven types of sex that symbolize the bond you've developed. For now, celebrate your progress, benefiting not just your marriage but your entire family.

Remember that each rung builds on the ones before it, creating a strong and virtuous cycle of marital intimacy. The more you engage in connected conversations, fun dates, and passionate intimacy, the more vibrant and fulfilling your relationship becomes. Embrace each step of this journey without fixating on the end goal. Sex is not the goal; it's a sign of success. Don't forget this.

"You don't get the checkered flag until you're consistent on the track."

There will be setbacks and unexpected rejections, but these moments are opportunities to reinforce your power, impact, adaptability, and, ultimately, your Man in Control. Over time, this approach will shift her perception of you from "You only care about sex" to recognizing your broader impact, leading to more open and positive interactions.

Anxiety Training:

I toyed with many ways to describe my anxiety training in a way that would motivate you to tackle it right now. I also asked many of my mentors and Lords in my program for their opinions. Unfortunately, the consensus was clear:

"Reading it would only deter you from using it."

I conquered the anxiety that the Insecurity Monster used to feed my beast: anger and extreme rage. I trained myself, and I did this without pills. I demanded myself to deal. If you struggle with insecurities, anxiety, and STAT Responses, I strongly suggest you go to https://MorrowMarriage.com/Tools and begin this training immediately.

LOVER'S LIST

- YOU ARE SO BEAUTIFUL
- YOUR PERSONALITY IS SO BEAUTIFUL
- YOU MAKE ME LAUGH
- NO MATTER HOW DOWN I AM, YOUR LAUGHTER LIGHTS ME UP
- WHEN THE SUN HITS YOUR EYES, I GET LOST IN THEM
- WHENEVER I FEEL LOST, WE FIND OUR WAY TOGETHER
- I DIDN'T KNOW WHAT LOVE WAS, BUT AS I LOVE YOU MORE EVERY DAY, I TRULY GET IT
- I GET TO SPEND THE REST OF MY LIFE WITH YOU
- I LOVE YOUR BRAIN
- I MARRIED THE MOST INTELLIGENT WOMAN ON THE PLANET
- I LOVE HOW YOU ALWAYS LEARN SOMETHING NEW
- WHEN YOU LEARNED ABOUT PARENTING, YOU INSPIRED ME TO BE A BETTER FATHER
- I APPRECIATE YOUR DISCERNMENT WITH MY FAMILY
- YOU MAKE GORGEOUS LITTLE BABIES. IF YOU'RE GONNA DO SOMETHING...
- I LOVE 'PRACTICING' EVEN THOUGH WE'RE NOT HAVING MORE BABIES
- THANK YOU FOR OUR CHILDREN.
- I APPRECIATE YOUR TEAMWORK AND YOUR PATIENCE WHEN I STRUGGLE WITH THE CHILDREN. YOU'RE AN INCREDIBLE MAMA

Connection over Correction Part I:

For many women, Words of Affirmation is at the top of their list of Love Languages. If you assess your history with gratitude, compliments, and affirmations–even empathy–it's likely not a record that fills you with pride. Some men stop expressing appreciation long before their wedding vows are exchanged, diminishing their wives' roles as partners and mothers.

"On a podcast episode, I expressed, 'It takes seven positives to outweigh one negative.' Kathryn immediately responded, "In a marriage, it takes 700.' Although 700 is a little much, this means it's go time."

It's essential to reverse this by building her up, improving the trajectory of your marriage through inspirational and masculine leadership. While we've discussed gratitude briefly in Ah Ha Moments, we're about to crank it up a level.

Gratitude must be both sincere and specific. For instance, if your wife cooks dinner, go beyond a simple "Thank you." Instead, acknowledge the effort and care she puts into the meal with something like, "Hey, Babe. Thank you for dinner. You're amazing. I appreciate how you take care of our family." This deeper level of appreciation significantly enhances your emotional connection.

Your "Lover's List" will be your playbook for expressing gratitude and creating a safe environment for your wife to open up and feel again. Men often resort to one-liners or superficial comments about their wives' looks or intelligence, mistaking them for meaningful compliments. These rarely hit the mark in making a wife feel truly valued or appreciated. If your wife is already expressing her frustration with your lack of connection, every time you fall short in this area, it adds a brick to the wall.

Saying, "Wow Babe, congratulations on the promotion. That's incredible! You've worked so hard for that— and so many hours! I'm so proud of you," strikes a chord of deep appreciation, unlike a weak, "Good job. Congrats on the promotion."

In moments of conflict or stress (SAFE Reactions), it's challenging to recall all the qualities you love, value, respect, and appreciate about your wife. The "Lover's List" is invaluable in reconditioning your mindset towards things you love about your wife. This list pulls you out of negative reactions more quickly and shortens the turnaround time after disagreements, keeping you honed in on the Green Light.

"This is even more important after bigger fights and altercations."

My Lover's List has been a game-changer for me and many men. One Mother's Day, I pulled out my Lover's List instead of just buying Kathryn a card or telling her what a great mom she is. I reviewed the things I had noticed over recent months:

- Kathryn's a great mom but always improving.
- Her dedication to parenting courses.
- Noticeable changes in the kids' responses to her.
- Her patience inspired me to be a better father.

From this list, crafting a heartfelt Mother's Day message was straightforward and impactful:

> ***"Happy Mother's Day Baby! You are the best mama on the planet. All the work that you've put in studying and learning how to become a better parent, I'm noticing it with the children and how much they look up to you and how much they adore you. I've also noticed I appreciate your***

leadership so much. I appreciate it because it inspires me to be a better father. Thank you."

Now, it's your turn. Open the notepad on your phone and start listing everything you value about your wife. Start without filtering—mention the physical attributes that attract you; that's usually the easiest. Then, allow the list to evolve into deeper, more meaningful qualities. You will quickly move to higher-level qualities as you tackle the ways you find her beautiful on the inside.

That's where the real, specific notes begin. Feel free to dive deep into your most recent conversation when you paused a TV show. Every detail has value and will add something to a situation down the road. Get excited as you do it. Note your feelings as you compile the list. Express those feelings when you refer to the list in the future.

"Let this run wild."

Gratitude isn't just a tool; it's a foundational element in a relationship that every "Man at Play" will learn to wield effectively. Start laying this foundation today. Express love, respect, and adoration to make your wife feel safe, seen, and appreciated. We'll dive deeper into this when we reach the Passion Pillar.

Sharing Your Feelings:

It's common for men to express their feelings defensively, often puking them, rather than sharing true feelings and, certainly, without validating their wife's emotions. Worse, many men are unaware of their true feelings, leading to counterproductive expressions that only add to the emotional barriers in a relationship. This phenomenon, where men struggle to identify and engage with their emotions, is so common that psychologists refer to it as Normative Male Alexithymia.

To truly connect with and validate your wife's emotions, you need a broader emotional vocabulary beyond just happy, sad, angry, and frustrated. Developing this emotional intelligence is essential for your personal satisfaction and becoming a fully engaged man.

"And your children need to learn this."

Dr. Gloria Wilcox's Feelings Wheel is a practical tool to help reframe your engagement with emotions. You can find resources to help you dive deeper at https://MorrowMarriage.com/Tools. It's crucial to not only identify your own emotions but process them with men until you are fluent in your wife's emotions, without assuming you know them. Before you can freely express your feelings, she must feel safe expressing hers. This includes experiencing the full spectrum of emotions, including positive ones like joy and excitement, and those that may induce the worst, like anxiety or fear.

"I'm not saying you cannot or are not allowed to feel. I am saying it's your wife's turn right now, and you have some learning to do."

Picture your wife rejecting your attempt at initiating sex. How do you feel? Often, the immediate reaction is "bad," but what lies beneath that superficial emotion? You might feel inadequate, which can undermine your sense of masculinity and trigger insecurity.

You feel lonely and unwanted or undesirable. These feelings might lead you to feel used for your contributions. You might unjustly assume that she is attracted to others, even suspecting infidelity, which could spiral into fears of divorce. Instead of confronting these fears directly, you might ask passive-aggressive questions about her activities or relationships. You might even be overtly aggressive with your accusations.

From my own experience, conflicts with Kathryn used to send me into a whirlwind of negative emotions—ashamed, hurt, sad, guilty, victimized, angry, vengeful. These emotions would drive bad decisions, perpetuating a destructive cycle. However, understanding and growing emotionally as a man is the first step toward breaking this cycle in your marriage and life.

"Emotions are the root of all success and all failure."

To control your reactions, you must first understand your feelings. This applies when considering your wife's emotions as well. While women are generally better at identifying their emotions, your wife might also be dealing with underlying feelings that manifest as anger or frustration. Some of you will be dealing with her abuse.

Your primary goal should be to create a safe space for her to express her feelings freely without fear of retaliation. As you learn about your own emotions, you aim to manage your responses to maintain this safe environment, not to overwhelm her with puking again.

A simple framework from GS Youngblood's The Masculine In Relationship can guide your interactions: state an indisputable fact, then express the feeling. When flipped, you might ask, "How do you feel when I [specific action]?" After she shares her feelings, listening attentively and responding appropriately is important, showing that you can be her steadfast support, even during emotional storms.

"STAT, STAT, and more STAT."

These aren't easy conversations; some will be necessary for both of you to move past lingering issues. However, instead of dwelling on the past—a common pitfall in therapy—focus on taking action in the present to demonstrate your responsibility and commitment as a man.

"Always think, future paced. You don't have to change your name like I did, but do what the 'new you' would do."

Actions often speak louder than words and can rapidly impact rebuilding safety, trust, and intimacy. To ensure you move your marriage forward, use your STAT Responses. Remember, any situation can promote positive emotional connections. If your wife excels in a test or on a day out with the kids as a mama, use those moments to encourage her to share her feelings. Always remind her of the positive emotions associated with you and your actions." How do you feel after [specific event]?"

Effective communication also reminds your wife of your commitment to this new emotional direction. Ask open-ended questions about her feelings in various scenarios and actively listen to her responses. For instance, during a pleasant conversation, you might ask, "How do you feel right now...after laughing like that?" This encourages her to share and helps you connect on a deeper, positive level.

Finally, when your wife begins to inquire about your feelings, use Youngblood's formula: state the fact and attach the feeling. For example, "When the kids scream at me, I feel frustrated and like I'm a bad dad." Then shut up. Let her process your words without further explanation. This approach will help her see you as a man who can express his needs and emotions responsibly, which will help her rediscover her natural, loving, empathetic, and nurturing self.

Don't Puke Your Feelings:

I have referenced this many times already. The right time for sharing your feelings will eventually arrive, but that time is not now. Resist the urge to undermine your progress by prematurely unloading all the emotions you're beginning to understand onto your wife. These uncontrolled outbursts of misunderstood, misidentified, and misdirected feelings only fortify the emotional barriers between you.

"When you embrace that your needs will be (more than) met by meeting your wife's—needs you didn't know you ever had—you will go from low to high, and you won't feel the need to unload."

You're working toward decades of reciprocal happiness in your relationship. She will, eventually, be genuinely curious about your feelings. This foundation is built on her freedom to express her emotions without fear of your typical SAFE Reactions.

You might feel disrespected, demeaned, or emasculated at times. It's crucial to approach these feelings correctly, as failing to do so won't resolve these emotions or bring you closer to the intimacy you desire in your marriage. Defensive reactions, where you dump your emotions on your wife instead of using the tools outlined, do more harm than good. You end up lecturing about your needs, whining, or blaming, which are all ways of protecting yourself without conscientiously conveying your feelings. When you feel disrespected, demeaned, or emasculated, you're taking it all too personally. If it hurts, you need to resolve the trigger deep within you.

"You're the fat guy that doesn't like it when people call him fat. Do something about it, Fatty."

Regardless, patience is key. When the appropriate time comes, remember the formula: state the indisputable fact, then attach the feeling. Be aware that your emotions might trigger a SAFE Reaction from her. You must use your STAT responses and continue structuring your momentum forward. Early tests will be frequent. For example, if she undermines you in front of friends, the old you might react aggressively, listing every grievance. Instead, evolve past your old patterns and calmly express, "Hey, Babe, when you contradict the details of the story I'm telling our friends, I feel undermined, disrespected, and unloved."

"Just don't do it if she's holding you accountable for your lies intertwined in the story."

Your calm but gentle assertiveness might initially be met with anger and emotion. However, as you consistently lead with understanding and clarity, her responses will begin to change. The end goal is when she says, "Baby, I never even thought about how that would make you feel. Of course, that feels terrible. I love you so much." This opens up a pathway to reinforce your relationship as you agree to focus on building each other up.

Be aware that insecurities can manifest in various scenarios, such as anxiety over your wife's phone use or why she's wearing sexy underwear. Rather than losing control and accusing her of an affair, calmly state your feelings, "Hey, babe, when you're on your phone while we're together, I feel insecure. I'm nervous about where we're at right now." Then shut up. Allow her to process and respond, but be ready with your STAT Responses if needed.

"30 seconds will feel like 3 hours. Let her process."

Many of you have tried therapy with mixed feelings about the process and results. It's crucial to remember that your wife might have felt similarly engaged in the past when you weren't as involved. Recognize this as a chance to extend grace and respond appropriately. If she doesn't participate in therapy assignments, express your feelings clearly without falling into old habits, "Honey, when we have homework from therapy, and you don't engage, I feel alone and scared for our future."

Finally, avoid asking, "What's wrong?" when she's in a bad mood. This question can come across as needy or desperate, especially if it is not timed right. Instead, address specific behaviors and how they make you feel: "Hey Babe, when you're frustrated and short with the kids, I feel frustrated too." This approach avoids the pitfalls of emotional dumping and paves the way for a deeper connection.

"This pissed Kathryn off initially. Now, she's grateful and apologizes when her actions don't align with the mama she wants to be without me using STAT. She holds herself accountable."

As you refine these communication techniques, the goal is to create an environment where your wife feels safe enough to reciprocate emotionally—so we can move to conversations. This involves consistent effort and patience initially, but the payoff is a relationship where both of you feel understood and valued and can handle emotional challenges together. You lift each other.

"This only happens with conversations, not communication."

Connection over Correction Part II:

John and Julie Gottman developed The Gottman-Rapoport Intervention as a blueprint for resolving relationship conflict. Within their model, the couple picks a topic over which conflict exists. One person assumes the role of speaker, and the other listens. The goal is for the listener to fully understand the speaker's position before the roles are reversed. It's an incredible tool that inspired Kathryn to develop the "Half-Rap." This is a one-way conflict intervention, as opposed to the proposed two-way model of Rapoport.

"A Half Rap is the first 'T' in STAT on steroids. You are NOT happy wife, happy lifein' it. You allow her to run you off the track, but you will keep driving your line."

With a half-rap, your goal is to listen to your wife. You will ask her questions, listen to her answers, summarize them in your own words as you understand them, and validate accordingly. You're trying to (actually) understand your wife, love her through it, and empathize to ensure she feels safe to share everything. This is not a tool to pull out during a date. It's more appropriate after a major event, disagreement, or point of conflict comes up.

Start by asking to open the discussion: "Hey, Babe, I've been reflecting on something from the other day. I'd like to ask you some questions." You only continue if she gives the green light to proceed. If not, you need to schedule it. Do not drop the bomb and run with it. Kathryn would tell you to always schedule it so that both parties have an opportunity to reflect on the subject matter prior to the conversation. However, Lords know how to STAT. [Wink Wink].

Your first question is simply: "How do/did you feel when [blank]? Or how do/did you feel about [blank]? Fill in the blank with the topic you're discussing. If you've got a particularly painful past fueled by conflict, a less intrusive alternative could be, "What do you think about [blank]? Regardless, once she speaks, you listen. You're not even validating yet; you're listening.

Here's an example that cuts right to an issue you've probably screwed up many times: "How do you feel when I get pouty and frustrated when we don't have sex?" Just let her process her thoughts and share. When she is done and pauses naturally, you're ready for your follow-up question.

"If I understand you correctly, [summarize her feelings in your own words as you understand them.]" Within the context of your pouting, she might say that she feels like a failure as a wife and that she can never make you happy. Respond with empathy as you say, "If I understand you correctly, you feel guilty and like you're a bad wife? She may clarify further. Keep confirming that you understand and ask questions to deepen your understanding. Once you've confirmed your understanding of her feelings, validate with empathy: "That must feel so frustrating for you. That must feel so terrible."

"And if you're getting her, you should be understanding how shitty she feels."

Once you get good at this, you and your wife will blast through this exercise in five minutes. If your marriage has been anywhere near as toxic as ours was, buckle up because this will take some time. You are about to find out exactly how much your wife has bottled up as you made her feel unsafe to share her true feelings. Initially, this will take longer for her to process, but I want you to embrace the time together. No matter how difficult it is for you. Maintain your cool and appreciate that she is processing through triggers that have been buried for years. You cannot defend, explain, or justify yourself.

"You have ZERO latitude for SAFE Reactions during these conversations. This is not about you; it's about your wife."

Down the road, you will have an opportunity to share your feelings, too. Even if she invites you to share, I encourage you to wait to take that step. You are not ready, and she still needs to follow your lead. I have adapted the Half-Rap so that you will add STAT at the end when you reframe the entire conversation.

"Do not get rattled if your perception doesn't match your wife's. Validation is not the same as agreement. Let your wife feel."

Your next question: "What do you need, Babe?" You can be less intrusive here again if needed. If your wife became upset or frustrated through the last question, you might say, "What would you like now to move forward?" You can create a natural way for her feelings to flow.

She might say, "I need you to stop whining and pouting. I need you to be a man. Why can't you date me more?"

Whatever she says, understand it and affirm it. When she opens up, and it's authentic, she's giving you the keys to the kingdom. "Wow, babe, that sucks. Of course, you need that. You know I can appreciate that a hundred percent. I understand why you wish I would date you more and flirt more before I try to initiate sex." Whatever she says, you appreciate, understand, and validate where she's at.

The last question digs deep into her true emotions and turns the focus from the painful past to the possible future. "How would you feel if you got what you wanted?" or, "How would you feel if you got what you needed?" You have already validated how she feels; now you want to provide structure for positive feelings and where you're structuring the marriage to go. "If I understand correctly, Babe, you would feel pressure lifted off you? The weight of the world would be off you? You'd feel more like we were a team?" Whatever she tells you.

Now, if she does begin negatively spiraling, cussing you out, or complaining again, you'd say, "I can appreciate why you'd feel that way for sure," but immediately pivot to the direction you are trying to lead. Add: "It must be so frustrating that I didn't talk to you for three days, and I didn't get your coffee for a few days when I was upset because we didn't have sex." Followed immediately by: "If I do understand correctly, you wouldn't even feel all that pressure if I don't shut down, dich my responsibility, and acted more grown up?"

Empathize with what she told you, then get permission and ask, "Is it possible for one more question?" If she's ready: "Is this tied to anything from the past?" At this point, she might go wild. Remember, the goal is to understand your wife. When she is done getting it all out, you will clarify in summary; then you will thank your wife. (After the summary), "Thank you Baby, I really appreciate how you opened up and shared this all with me."

Once you've completed the process, you STAT. When we do our training and role-play on Half Rap calls with Kathryn, I add STAT to the experience and suggest, for example, taking her hand, acting cute, and doing the summarization as I show her the new direction.

"Kathryn loves the STAT addition. Remember, direction for the future."

"While reflecting on my past actions to release my guilt and shame, I realized that everything I had released my wife for was a direct result of the actions that I carry guilt and shame for. As a result, I realized I had only my judgment to release. Then there was nothing left but myself, my actions, and to look at them openly and honestly so I could make a change."---Rob Richardson, USA: Mentor To Lords.

"Fuck this is powerful—Been there."

Releasing Shame:

Your path to becoming a Man with Impact must include releasing the shame holding you back. This realization became clear after working with many men burdened by past mistakes. When burdened by shame and guilt over past failures, you cannot detach from the triggers that bind you to SAFE Reactions. Whether it's the programming from your parents or your past sins, your ability to respond as your best, most authentic self requires this step.

Reflect on the ways you've stacked shame throughout your life. Consider the coping mechanisms you've adopted to avoid facing your internal struggles. How many are there? Whether these actions were significant or small, if you feel guilty or ashamed of how you acted in your relationships or other areas of your life, it's time to confront them, examine them, and then let them go.

"You only know what you know when you know it."

Give yourself the grace to rise from the past and lead your marriage into the future. You are not alone in this struggle. I struggled with severe anger issues. I abused Kathryn physically, emotionally, and sexually. I've wrestled with addiction and faced tremendous guilt over how I treated my children from previous relationships.

I made the painful choice to move away from my son from a previous relationship. Some reasons make sense to me, but still, I had to revisit shame. Similarly, I stopped a legal battle for another child so Kathryn and I could budget the funds to start our own family with in vitro fertilization for Briar, Vale, and Riddick. I felt tremendous shame over this.

"Shame. No matter how happy we are, I cannot let lingering thoughts tear down the fortune I have with my family now."

I also had to sever ties with my adoptive father, mother, siblings, or the rest of my extended family due to their toxic behavior. Despite the dramatic improvements in my life, that left me with deep-seated guilt for years. Are they entirely to blame? I know I could have handled things differently with the knowledge I have now, but I also understand that they were not prepared to grow as I have. It was the best decision given the circumstances. I released the shame and guilt for these significant events and no longer looked back.

Shame, guilt, and regret keep you playing in your pain, preventing you from fully embracing your potential. These feelings can surface sharply, especially as you begin comprehending the depth of your actions and their impacts on your loved ones. Ruminating on the man you were before your changes can force you into severe lows. I could write a whole book for what I have been ashamed of.

"If that was my focus, we would not be disrupting divorce now. I would be divorced."

To grow and move forward, you have to consider the impact you want to make and embrace the control you have over your development and growth. Bring your regrets and weaknesses into the open and connect with other men with similar challenges and journeys. No matter what it involves - infidelity, abusive behavior, familial issues, or professional setbacks - it's crucial to let go of these burdens. It si important to point out that you must do this with of men that either have, or are in the process of learning, the skills you need. Anyone you are learning from should have or be striving for the same or higher level of growth as you are.

"You are responsible for your choices. Regardless, you cannot do anything about your past choices. Rise up."

This is not a one-time event but an ongoing journey of reflection and growth. Each time you read through this book, or each session of self-reflection helps you dive deeper and distance yourself further from past pain. Your shame acts as an anchor; releasing it empowers you to move toward the future you want.

There's no need to feel ashamed of past mistakes and failures born out of ignorance. Many of these failures were due to a lack of resources, poor role models, or negative influences in your life. Now, you are overcoming your mistakes. Actively working through these challenges will pave the path for the New Man, the new you, with every step.

"It's not your fault for the mistakes you've made as a broken man, but they are your responsibility. It is your fault if you don't become the man you were born to be now."

The Partnership Pillar

Partnership

Having laid the foundation of your Peace Pillar at home, the next crucial step involves nurturing and sustaining that peace through a solid partnership. This stage is critical and should not be rushed into with the expectation that friendship and passion will instantly follow. These are outcomes of the Passion Pillar, set in place once a solid partnership is formed again. The partnership itself is built on the principles of being a Man in Control, Man at Home, and Man with Kids.

Man in Control enhances what you've learned in the Peace Pillar. Remember the opening lines of this book that challenged your victim mentality? Here, you'll learn to make decisions that align you and your marriage with your core values. It's time to move beyond the "Nice Guy" persona that has blinded you. This persona isn't something your wife created, nor can she dismantle it for you. This section is about transforming into the best, most authentic version of yourself, free from the confines of the Nice Guy Triangle.

"You need to look in the mirror to conquer your Nice Guy."

A Man at Home is actively and positively involved in domestic life. I will provide practical steps that help you demonstrate reliability and trustworthiness in your home. Your wife needs to trust herself when she depends on you, and this goes far beyond merely providing a safe space. The Partnership Pillar is about teamwork, showing up for each other in ways that create a deep connection, eliminating all doubt that your wildest dreams can only be achieved together.

Man with Kids escalates the commitment to the future. You're not just roommates or business partners, and certainly not enemies—as Kathryn and I once were. It's challenging for your wife to maintain opposition or hostility towards a man who embodies a safe, partnering presence. Remember, you're not merely 'helping out' at your wife's home. Chores like dishes and laundry are responsibilities regardless of who you live with or for how long. Similarly, caring for your children is not babysitting; it's parenting. Release any sense of entitlement for doing what should be routine and fully embrace your role as a partner in the most rewarding relationship of your life. Doing so will inspire your wife to engage in the partnership with the same level of commitment and enthusiasm.

"Kathryn encourages women to 'relax' and let a man 'help,' but the sensitivity of the word (to women) is something you should be aware of. Therefore, I encourage men to let go of 'helping' to become involved."

MAN IN CONTROL

Act like you just got laid.

Man in Control

Many of you have never honestly had the opportunity to develop authentic confidence. Some of you approach the world with genuine confidence; however, you cannot maintain it at home. I used to be incredible at faking confidence in business and life, but Kathryn saw right through it.

The path to developing true confidence as a man can involve some harmful roadblocks, including glorified dating advice that fails to enhance a sustainable, long-term relationship. The superficial allure promoted by such advice does not match the genuine attraction that comes from consistently presenting the true, authentic version of yourself—when you truly believe in and love yourself.

"You cannot fake it 'till you make it. Your wife knows you better than anyone else."

When you align your actions with your core values, the transformation is universally evident. Your colleagues, friends, and employees will notice the change. Your children will respect and follow you more willingly, and your wife will inevitably see the most significant difference. When faced with challenges, you won't shrink back or defensively shield yourself from anyone's judgments—instead, you will respond with natural, confident leadership. Remember your STAT training.

Ask yourself: Do you truly know who you are and what you stand for? I will guide you through identifying your core values while showing you the path I took to define my own. Drifting through life without a clear set of values leads to reactive behavior that results in adjusting your actions to suit your wife's mood so you can avoid conflict. This always makes things worse and never really resolves the underlying issues.

This section gives you the tools to learn how to make decisions in every aspect of your life, reaching far beyond your relationship with your wife. By applying and understanding your core values, you'll discover how to eradicate "bad" habits while establishing a framework for making clear decisions. This framework will provide direction and structure, enabling you to confidently move forward regardless of how your wife or anyone else might react. This is not just about asserting control but embracing a leadership role that naturally emerges from living authentically according to your values.

Control by Your Core Values:

There's far too much advice encouraging you to "fake it 'til you make it." It fails to address the essence of genuine confidence: understanding who you are, what you stand for, and applying those values consistently in your life. True confidence flows naturally when your core values guide you. It's important to recognize that while your values inevitably impact your wife, they originate from your beliefs and actions.

Interestingly, my wife Kathryn and I have our own, unique core values and have only occasionally discussed them at length. It's unnecessary because it's possible that your wife may not have defined her core values at all, but your role is to continually be yourself. This authenticity makes you a leader at home and in the world. This man disrupts the old norms and sets new standards.

"Think about how I am #DisruptingDivorce"

Feel free to adopt my core values, modify them, or develop your own. It's crucial that you deeply believe in whatever values you choose. They should transcend your roles— as a husband, father, or professional—and capture the core of who you are. If you're unclear about your underlying values, you cannot truly lead yourself, let alone anyone else.

Integrity: I am a diamond.

Am I flawless? Far from it. I make mistakes. Yet, I must stay true to my word, acknowledge my errors, learn from them, and consistently act in alignment with my true direction. Integrity is a cornerstone of this book, The Reset, and Lords; it's fundamental to self-belief and confidence.

Transparency: Live like a window.

Integrity doesn't shield you from errors; it compels you to own them openly. Unlike the "Nice Guys" who conceal their flaws to gain approval, I choose transparency. I openly acknowledge my mistakes transparently, which is essential for real growth.

"If I have a relapse or, as Kathryn calls it, a 'Narc Out' today, I'll tell you about it on my podcast tomorrow."

Energy: The energy of a Puppy.

Energy is infectious, and I aim to bring positive, vibrant energy into every situation. This shift in perspective was a game-changer for me, particularly in how I interact with my family compared to my clients. Assessing and adjusting my energy levels helps me maintain this vitality in all aspects of my life.

Love: Love like a wolf; protect and serve.

Becoming self-centered requires no effort at all in the hustle of life. It's also very easy to default our attention to the "now" and ignore everything else to become self-centered. For example, "I need to work." But the real strength lies in protecting and serving those we care about. My bond with my wife is strengthened when I make her a priority by genuinely serving her. Doing this creates and nurtures a mutual respect and love that makes our bond unbreakable.

Consistency: Take the Oscar Home. (Act like you just got laid).

Consistency is perhaps the most important value. Without it, you can't maintain any other core value. It's about keeping your chosen persona regardless of external circumstances. This isn't about "faking it" but embodying resilience and stability, regardless of life's challenges, from personal rejections to professional setbacks.

"You would not care about so many little details if you just got laid. You would not take everything so personally. You'd take the Oscar home."

Start by crafting your Core Values List and making it part of your daily life. Engage with it, use it, and live it. Reflect on your actions from the previous day and align today's decisions with your values. Keep your list concise; an overly complex list can cloud your focus. When each value lives and resonates deeply within you, they will guide your decisions and actions. An example for me is that I love the Lords, but not like I love Kathryn. But I can love like a wolf with my wife and the Lords.

One of my mentors, Cole Dasilva, @coleluisdasiliva, taught a valuable lesson during a special bonus call for Lords: Your core values must be measurable. Ask yourself some important questions: Can you assess your values with a daily review? Are you able to measure them during your morning routine? Can you set a goal to be 1% better today on each value?

If you struggle, choose core values you can assess and flip to become 100% better. Many men pick arbitrary values such as, "I'll be better every day," and have no real way to assess their values. To make this easier to integrate for the Nice Guy, I purposefully keep it binary, "Was I or was I not?" I was either integral, transparent, energetic, loving, and consistent, or I was not.

THE NICE GUY TRIANGLE

Approval | Expectations | Hiding | Keeping Score

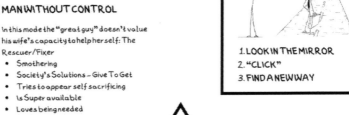

1. LOOK IN THE MIRROR
2. "CLICK"
3. FIND A NEW WAY

MAN WITHOUT CONTROL

In this mode the "great guy" doesn't value his wife's capacity to help herself: The Rescuer/Fixer

- Smothering
- Society's Solutions – Give To Get
- Tries to appear self sacrificing
- Is Super available
- Loves being needed

MAN WITHOUT IMPACT

In this mode the "great guy" doesn't value his wife's views or feelings: The Persecutor.

- Angry (openly and passively)
- Aggressive
- Judgmental
- Bullying
- Demanding
- Spiteful and vindictive

A MAN WITHOUT POWER

In this mode the "great guy" doesn't value himself and projects on his wife: The Victim.

- Manipulative
- 'Poor me' syndrome
- Helpless, desperate and needy
- Pouty or complaining
- Blame Push, Shame Dump, Guilt Throw

"Despite all the obstacles I thought stood in my way, I was the only one that really held me back. Conquering the Nice Guy within changed everything for me."---Pete O'Reilly, USA: Mentor To Lords.

Understanding The Nice Guy Triangle:

It's common for men to choose wives who reinforce their worst habits and complement their weaknesses. This also perpetuates the dysfunctional behaviors ingrained throughout our lives—relationships like this fuel codependency and all the patterns and dynamics that come with it. There's no need to fall into the depths of toxicity or abuse as I once did.

Unchecked SAFE Reactions erode your future. Intentionally embodying the role of a confident, proactive leader can redirect your life's course. You must embrace the confidence needed to embrace your capacity to lead fully. Remember, this is a willful choice, a decision to become a New Man, not a pick-and-choose quick fix.

"I don't know why we say, 'Repeat the cycle.' The cycle gets worse with every rotation."

Becoming a Man in Control:

Armed with the knowledge and skills of a Man in Power and a Man with Impact, the time has come to move beyond following the pace car. Embrace your core values and step into Man in Control. This transition is critical for conquering your limiting Nice Guy persona and genuinely advancing toward the life you envision.

"You'll never live your core values if you're stuck in the victim triangle."

No matter how you were raised, every man can succumb to these pitfalls when he and his wife are disconnected, especially when there is a lack of physical intimacy. Feeling unwanted by your partner can be emasculating, undermining your confidence and triggering your SAFE Reactions that perpetuate a destructive cycle. It's essential to recognize and break this cycle, to step back and understand how you navigate this disgusting triangle, as this awareness is your first step toward true empowerment.

"Something happens to a man when his wife just doesn't want him."

Why you are in the triangle is irrelevant. You must step out.

1. Man without Control

The Man without Control faces a dire predicament as he sits at the pinnacle of the Triangle. Once control is lost, the only remaining direction is downward—there is no ascent from this point. This position erodes any impact and power you might have painstakingly built. Actions taken from this state do not reflect the "Great" man you perceive yourself to be. Instead, these actions undermine every positive change you've strived to achieve. During these moments, your reality is skewed, and you feel like a victim, providing fertile soil to blame your wife and justify your anger when she reacts.

"When you're a Man without Control, your wife becomes your only why: your reason."

Like a master "fixer," you'll build a pedestal for your wife, put her on it, and then begin to treat her like a queen who deserves the world. When conflicts arise, you resort to Society Solution band-aids like "happy wife, happy life" or other simplistic fixes that only exacerbate the transactional nature of your efforts. Your wife feels these efforts not as genuine gestures, but as covert contracts oozing with your hidden expectations.

"As you give to get, your expectations bleed out of you. Your pouting, frustrations or anger intensify."

As your unmet expectations stack, you will inadvertently smother your wife. She may demand space. A request you are neither equipped to understand nor provide. She will believe your changes are insincere and aimed solely at appeasing her, elevating her further on her pedestal. She becomes neither your partner nor your equal, but an unattainable ideal.

When your constant quest for validation and approval fails, your disappointment leads you to emotional outbursts or withdrawal. This cycle begs the question—how can she genuinely reciprocate when she's placed so high on a pedestal and boxed in by your needs? You are left asking, "Don't I deserve better?" You reinforce the walls that keep you isolated and misunderstood.

2. Man without Impact

When you are fully entrenched in chaos, you've transitioned into a Man without Impact. You've lost all control. Here, your potential to effect positive change rapidly diminishes. Rather than nurturing and protecting, you find yourself critiquing her flaws and efforts, fueled by a slew of unmet expectations that have only entrenched your sense of entitlement. Leadership eludes you, and you're stuck where you can't lead yourself or your wife. As you slide down within the Nice Guy Triangle, you eventually lose the power to influence any aspect of your relationship positively.

"By not accepting your love, her disapproval sends you deep into a low."

Examine your state: It's frustrating to work so hard and spend so much of your energy to see little progress or acceptance from your wife. Frustrations build, and you are convinced she does not try like you try. You believe you're communicating effectively and keeping your cool under pressure. Yet, the real issues remain unaddressed, and the emotional connection seems so far away.

"You feel like you're in constant negotiation for her affection, and she's holding your love hostage."

Reflect on this dynamic: the weight of your needs—which she cannot fulfill—creates unbearable pressure on her, making every step with you a potential minefield. Each expectation you set builds a barrier between you, fortifying the walls that keep her at a safe distance from you. You are no longer the 'loving' man or 'Nice Guy' you said you were. Your wife is forced to lay boundaries to protect herself.

"How else is she going to stay safe?"

Confront the harsh truth: she feels trapped by the immense wall of your needs and expectations, which causes her to dread the emotional fallout from the simplest interactions. She is so afraid to engage with you that she hides her most authentic self, seeking safety from your demands.

"Lose your expectations."

Consider the impact of keeping score: this habit fuels your dissatisfaction and feeds into a cycle of resentment and anger. This resentment doesn't endear you to her; rather, it showcases you as the villain, distancing her further. Each bid you make or deed that goes unseen adds up in your mind, and when the tally gets critical, it comes out in hostility, a manifestation of your worst self.

"If you haven't already, start your Lover's List instead."

This journey isn't merely about managing your relationship dynamics; it's a present decision to explore self-leadership and integrity across all facets of life. When your daily life aligns with your core values, everyone around you will see your transformation. Everyone will see this new you: your family, coworkers, your friends, and most of all, your wife. Beyond improving your marriage, embracing this path to authentically lead by example demonstrates a steadfast commitment to growth and self-understanding.

2b. Moving from Man without Impact to Man without Power

Negatively, keeping a score prevents you from genuinely offering love. You may believe your wife should automatically love, adore, respect, and constantly crave your presence. You don't see the truth behind her denial of reciprocation. Your 'unwavering love and attention' lacks genuine connection and does not allow her the freedom to express her true feelings without fear.

This mindset creates a transactional love where you give only to get, yet your needs remain unmet even when you receive love in this exchange. This is a Man without Impact who begins to diminish his self-worth, gradually withdrawing from her needs and desires, questioning why he should cater to her when his love is unrequited.

Your frustration eventually morphs into aggression. You are no longer the protector or provider; you become the persecutor, letting anger and resentment dictate your actions. This hostility makes you demanding and spiteful, neglecting your responsibilities and daily tasks.

"After all, she can get her own coffee, right? She doesn't do anything for you."

As a Man without Control, you might feel disproportionately hurt by this turmoil. Remember, fairness is irrelevant; effectiveness is what matters. Embracing self-love and self-validation allows you to maintain your impact without needing external approval. This shift enables you to support your wife's journey away from SAFE Reactions, using STAT Responses as guiding principles.

"When you learn how to fill your cup with Morrow Momentum, the only feeling that can describe it is FREEDOM."

As a Man without Impact, your initial reaction might be to protect yourself. If you're not overtly disengaging or sulking, you may deliver subtle, passive-aggressive comments as she passes. Think about the times your sullen disposition clouded the room when she showed disinterest or when your awkwardness in conversations felt crippling.

"A Man without Impact will make an impact. He will push his wife away slowly over time until she coasts, cheats, or wants a separation or divorce."

You've seen this play out before. In seeking approval in unconventional ways, you validate your worth at your wife's emotional expense. You internalize this as you note her apparent lack of enthusiasm toward you while insisting (in your mind) that she should openly and continually express her love.

Convinced of your worth and cloaked in your self-righteousness, you hide behind the facade of the man you once admired in the mirror. Caught in this cycle, you repeat outdated strategies and nurture a growing sense of entitlement rather than creating genuine intimacy and mutual respect.

Embracing change requires confronting these patterns and asking, "What could I do differently? My way hasn't worked for years. Why would I want to do that now?" Escaping from this cycle demands more than acknowledgment; it demands your unequivocal decision to redefine your interactions and eliminate expectations in life so that your core values drive your actions.

3. Man Without Power

A Man without Power caught within the triangle will say, "I've been giving and giving. I'm trying to fix the whole marriage all by myself." Your wife's disapproval weighs—she's driving right over you—which in turn fuels your fears and feelings of worthlessness and failure. This gives way to shame and robs you of your power.

Sadly, you're often only aware this is happening once it's too late. As these feelings grow, you begin to inadvertently throw your guilt onto your wife and start leveraging your frustration, anger, and resentment as tools to make her feel guilty for not loving you in the way you deserve. You repeatedly point out your loving contributions, pleading, "Why don't you just love me?"

"Your wife is becoming your why not—your reason to quit."

In this powerless state, the concept of impact shifts dramatically. You might challenge your wife's emotions and motives by questioning her understanding and labeling her reactions as overreactions. "Why does she continue to feel misunderstood?" "How can she be so insensitive?" These questions highlight a deep-seated frustration that is not about her distance but your internal battle. You become the architect of your discontent, turning the blame towards her as she grows weary of the constant pressure and emotional walls you build.

"You cannot love her one moment, then turn to hate and blame in the next, and still expect her to love, or even like, you in return."

If your wife attempts to engage, the environment you've created transforms it into a no-win situation. In this catch-22, your emotional defenses swiftly shut down any attempt at openness. Your emotional abuse keeps her affection and her respect away. The (lack of) power you wield over your emotions starts to define her reactions toward you. As she pulls away, it's not merely a rejection of affection but a defensive mechanism protecting her against the emotional turmoil you impose.

"You are responsible for your choices. You need to step out of the triangle."

Recognizing this dynamic is critical. Your actions and reactions within this triangle undermine your sense of self and perpetuate a cycle of emotional hell that keeps both of you locked in a dance of dissatisfaction and misunderstanding. It's imperative to understand that you can change this narrative, step away from the victim mentality, and reclaim the role of a proactive, empowering partner. This step requires acknowledging your part in the dynamic and choosing a path of personal growth and emotional maturity.

Exiting the Nice Guy Triangle:

Escaping from the slavery of the Nice Guy Triangle begins with confronting the harsh reality that you feel powerless. This sensation of powerlessness manifests by beating yourself up and throwing yourself into the depths of shame and self-doubt. "Why can't she love me?" "Why doesn't she see I have so much love to give?" You're blinded, closed to the real reasons why she cannot return her love. This internal dialogue leads you to invalidate your worth and traps you in a cycle of pain and self-destruction.

"You no longer have hope, you no longer smile, you sit and brood in silence."

Embracing a narrative of powerlessness is a choice. Your SAFE Reactions and powerless mindset are not set in stone; they require transformation. Remember, we cannot control or change our wives—this is a fundamental truth. You've never been truly powerless. The moment you understand that each decision you've avoided, each action you've shied away from, was to dodge the necessary work to embody a Man with Power, Impact, and Control, you're ready to start the essential self-work. This begins with an honest assessment of your emotions and reality.

"You can lie and tell yourself you're a Ferrari, or you can own that you're a Focus and do something about it."

Continuing as a Man without Power invariably leads to remaining a Man without Control. You can never blame your wife for your lack of control over your emotions or choices. Blaming your wife for your emotional responses or bad decisions only perpetuates your misery and powerlessness. Acknowledge that your true power was never lost, you suppressed it.

"Until now, you were never allowed to wield your own power."

Embracing Your Power:

Believing in yourself and the transformative impact of this belief is monumental. You become the best man for the job, the husband your wife desires, the leader she respects. This self-belief propels you to live as a Man in Control, taking the Oscar home. You will manage most situations with confidence, even when it feels overwhelming. Fear has no place here. The monster is destroyed. Gaining control over yourself, the beast hides from you. With a clear mission to provide, protect, and cherish, your goal is not perfection but to create the best possible environment for a thriving marriage.

"Then we identify your God-given purpose(s) and unleash the impact you were born to make."

Moving Forward:

As you ascend from the depths of the Triangle, you acknowledge your missteps—elevating your wife to an unattainable pedestal, expecting her to fulfill your every emotional void, and resenting her when she falls short.

"To conquer your Nice Guy, embrace your power, and take responsibility for your actions. Then lead with integrity and confidence."

The path out of the Nice Guy Triangle is paved with driven self-examination and an unrelenting commitment to personal growth. You are not just reinventing yourself but fortifying your marriage and paving the way to be the man you were born to be. This transformation is not just about personal fulfillment; it's about setting a rock-solid foundation for legacy. Your impact will transcend your life and influence the world for the better.

Reality Checks:

The Nice Guy Triangle often clouds your perception, distorting reality to justify your lack of control, impact, or power. To illustrate this and help you reflect in real time, I'll share two personal memories. You'll most likely need support beyond self-reflection, as mindset shifts are a significant component of The Reset. Since your wife is likely not on board, and while you're in the triangle, successful men often rely on additional peer support, like the Lords, to navigate these reality checks.

Reflective Stories for Reality Checking

1. The Street Crossing Incident: During a nighttime walk with Kathryn from a hotel to a store, she suggested we cross the street for safety—to see oncoming traffic. We argued over which side was safer, which escalated into a dispute until we entered the store. In frustration, I accused Kathryn of undermining my decisions, claiming she yelled at me for seven or eight minutes as we crossed the street.

   She calmly asked, "How long does it take to cross the street?" Realizing it only took a few seconds, I had to admit that her yelling—tied directly to the length of time in mind—did not align. I felt attacked. It was a story I made up in my mind. This episode highlighted how deeply I was entrenched in my distorted reality, as it caused me to feel emasculated over a simple suggestion from Kathryn.

   When feeling undermined, emasculated, or disrespected, your own reality often misleads you. Kathryn was right. It's always better to have traffic facing you when walking. I was SAFE Reacting because I felt stupid for not thinking about safety in the first place.

"Anyone has a right to discuss safety, and in that moment, I became more unsafe than any car hitting us."

2. The Gum Incident: While driving with Kathryn, I wanted to discard my chewing gum but hesitated to avoid hitting the car

next to us. When Kathryn offered to throw it out on her side, I irrationally snapped at her because I believed she was insinuating I was gross for holding the gum. This misunderstanding parallels the feelings you might experience when your wife pulls back from affection or intimacy. It exemplifies how fear of disapproval can warp your perceptions and reactions.

"Kathryn wanted to help me, and I missed an opportunity to connect."

This is an excellent opportunity to remind you of your Lover's list. There have been times when I've been so grateful for how Kathryn treated me—love, respect, gratitude, affirmations, even touch. Whenever we've had conversations about it, she always reminds me with a smile, a touch, and soft words that this is who she is. Although I know she's not perfect, and at times I do need to hold her accountable, she is pretty damn perfect now. I can check my reality with my Lover's List if I am in a low.

Challenges of Reality Checking:

These stories highlight the challenges of self-awareness and the importance of external support. Your wife might try to help you see reality, but if she does, it might only sometimes come across gently, or you might still need to be receptive to it. Moreover, her perceptions may be skewed by the dynamic you've both created. It's crucial to find support from those who genuinely want you to succeed—people who will straightforwardly tell you your faults, hold you accountable, and push you to grow without endorsing harmful behaviors or enabling denial.

"Proximity only matters with valuable people in proximity."

If you react defensively or feel unjustly victimized, you're likely deep in the Nice Guy Triangle. The problem is, you likely won't see it. The thousands of men I've helped would agree that when you're in a low, you're out of control. This can lead to a cycle of resentment and miscommunication, where your wife feels increasingly pressured and misunderstood. Get support from someone you trust.

When I had what Kathryn described as a "Narc Out," a relapse years after my last outburst, a trusted mentor, who I also mentored, helped me realign with reality. This accountability allowed me to meaningfully apologize to Kathryn, leading to the best conversation we've ever had without needing her to struggle with forgiveness. Kathryn trusts me and my sincerity. This shows the importance of applying and using the tools and support from The Reset while keeping open and honest conversation at the forefront.

Kathryn is also often there for me now, and I can use her tools to navigate reality checks safely. Although I can check my reality often or my turnaround time is rapid, my partner is my ally. It would be best if you had a very clear understanding and practiced allowing yourself this level of trust when your reality is skewed.

"Having strong, male help like Lords, who have the same tools and resources, is powerful as long as your wife cannot check your reality with you."

Stepping Out of the Triangle:

To truly step out of the Nice Guy Triangle and prevent repeating negative patterns, you must apply the principles taught in The Reset. This includes using reality checks, understanding your triggers, engaging in open conversation without being defensive, keeping score, or using covert contracts.

"Now that you are becoming your most authentic self, you absolutely cannot hide who you are."

As you continue to work through these processes, remember that transitioning from the old patterns to becoming a Man in Control involves continuous effort and dedication. Don't be discouraged by setbacks. See them as opportunities to strengthen yourself and deepen your understanding of yourself and your marriage. Becoming a Man in Control is challenging, but you will do it with persistence and support.

Approval and Validation:

Seeking approval and validation is a common trap, often manifesting in behaviors that undermine genuine connections. The need for external validation from your wife will distort the dynamics of your relationship, especially with intimacy. It's a harsh reality that many men equate sex with ultimate validation—feeling loved, validated, and valued when desired sexually by their wives. This perception stems from an internal void and broadcasts a message of dependency: "I don't feel like a man unless you have sex with me." This mindset not only diminishes your self-worth but also pressures your wife. Nothing good comes from this interaction.

Rethinking Sex as Validation:

Understanding that sex has been a crutch for validation allows us to begin deconstructing this behavior. Reflect on your actions—were they genuinely aimed at loving or healing your relationship, or were they attempts to feel better about yourself, gauged by your wife's willingness to engage sexually? Such motives will likely fail because they don't address the root issues, instead perpetuating the cycle of the Nice Guy Triangle. Each lap around the triangle leaves more scars.

"You're lighting your own car on fire."

Navigating the Rejection Ladder:

Consider your daily interactions and decisions, like coming home from work. If you're dreading another fight or hoping for sex, you're likely already compromising your authenticity to avoid conflict. This isn't just about preventing unpleasantness; it's about shielding yourself from feelings of inadequacy. This is precisely what prevents you from climbing the ladder.

When you manage to climb the ladder and still miss a higher rung, the inadequacy feeds the monster, and mistakes are made. This cycle often results in seeking her apology the morning after a conflict, not because you want to resolve the issue or prove you're right but to escape feelings of disapproval and unworthiness. Your wife's forced apology temporarily satisfies your need to have her acknowledge she was wrong to withhold her approval of you. This constant need for approval—or to avoid disapproval—leads to a lack of control, making it impossible to lead effectively in your home or live according to your true core values.

"You're not on my ladder, you're playing Snakes 'n Ladders, and you're the snake."

The Broader Impact of Approval-Seeking:

Your approval-seeking behavior doesn't just strain your marriage; it extends to other areas of life. I realized how my actions with my children or even home maintenance was driven by a desire for approval from others, not by a genuine desire to engage and do. I sought compliments from strangers at the park about how cute my kids were or maintained a spotless home for potential visitors in an attempt to avoid being judged. None of it was for my own satisfaction or personal desires.

"You need to dig deep."

From External to Internal Validation:

Exiting the triangle requires learning to validate yourself. We will investigate this further with Morrow Momentum. You will reclaim your power and authenticity by filling your own cup and making decisions rooted in your core values. This shift is crucial for personal fulfillment and establishing a healthy and balanced relationship where you and your wife feel loved, valued, and respected for who you truly are. When you learn to give without expectations, your marriage and life will be more abundant than you could ever dream.

Reflect on Covert Contracts - Giving to Get:

Recognizing and being mindful of the covert contracts you create is vital. These often-unspoken agreements set you up for disappointment and resentment because they place unfair expectations on your wife, creating undue pressure and emotional exhaustion. Seeing and dismantling these contracts is crucial for creating a reciprocal relationship.

The deep reflection required for this process, coupled with your willingness to change your behaviors, are powerful and the impact is amazing. Over time, the rewards include a more stable sense of self-worth and healthier interactions with those around you.

"From one Nice Guy to another, conquering equals freedom."

Expectations and Entitlement:

As you dive deeper into the Nice Guy Triangle, your feelings of inadequacy will intensify. In seeking approval from your wife, you might find yourself playing the role of a "Simp," the modern term for Nice Guy, desperately trying to earn validation. This desperation makes the approval you seek more elusive. When you give excessively, hoping to get something in return, your expectations turn to entitlements, impossible for anyone to meet. Since your self-worth relies heavily on external validation, failing to meet your entitled standards will lead to a loss of control and a distorted view of your value.

"In an effort to feel worthy, you will lose your power and hold everyone around you accountable with blame."

The Cycle of Expectations and Resentment:

Expectations can be described as premeditated resentments. When they are not met, they lead to feelings of unworthiness, compelling you to act out in ways that either diminish your impact or make you surrender your power in an attempt to prove your worth—really to yourself. This is when the blame-pushing, guilt-throwing, or shame-dumping begins. You avoid confronting your feelings of inadequacy by placing the responsibility on others.

Entitlement and Society's Misguided Solutions:

Society reinforces harmful entitlements of love, affection, respect, or sex, driving you to believe, "I provide, protect, I'm a great dad, I'm a great guy, I deserve." True entitlement should only extend to striving for personal goals and being the best and most authentic version of yourself—not demanding reciprocation of feelings or actions.

Navigating Expectations in Personal Development:

Many men engage in self-improvement programs to become their best selves but become resentful when their wives do not immediately follow suit and praise them. In their failure to reassess their expectations, they often wonder why their wives hesitate to engage intimately even though they have made significant personal progress. This misunderstanding can lead to impatience and renewed conflict.

"You cannot lead your wife if you cannot, first, lead yourself."

Balancing Expectations and Self-Satisfaction:

One of the most challenging steps in managing your expectations is learning that you are the one who needs to fill your own cup. This is done by being mindful of what you expect (from others and yourself) and being disciplined in using the skills learned from The Reset. You create a healthier dynamic in any relationship when you let go of your expectations and start focusing on being a giving, grateful, and loving man without strings attached. Until you are proud of the person you see in the mirror, can you genuinely claim to deserve love, respect, and passion, a reciprocal relationship?

"Relationships are valued. You are either valuable, or you are not."

Maintaining Your Progress:

To ensure that you are genuinely proud of who you are, it's vital to maintain the practices taught in The Reset and to check yourself regularly. Lords use an assessment, a scorecard, and other Lords to hold themselves accountable, available at https://MorrowMarriage.com/Tools.

Keeping expectations in check allows you to approach relationships and personal goals with a healthier mindset, preventing old, destructive patterns from re-emerging. This section reminds us that while self-improvement is critical, it must be approached with the right mindset that creates genuine self-worth and constructive, reciprocal relationships free from unrealistic expectations and entitlement.

"This is why you must become this man in and out of the marriage and exactly why you gain rapid momentum using Morrow Momentum."

Hiding and Filtering:

Navigating through the dynamics of the Nice Guy Triangle often means hiding your true self or filtering out the man you aspire to become. Walking on eggshells around your wife means concealing who you are. Similarly, when you're in SAFE Mode, you filter out the New Man you want to be, particularly when you shut down during conflicts. To break free from these patterns, start by grounding yourself in your core values and stepping out of your comfort zone. This approach will help you rebuild your lost confidence and establish a robust foundation at home.

I often say, "Get in her face without invading her space." This means asserting yourself while respecting her boundaries. When your wife demands space or rejects your advances, it's crucial to remain firm and use your core values to guide your STAT Responses. This will help you navigate conflicts with clarity and direction.

"Respect is earned in the disrespect, through your STAT Responses."

By staying true to your goals and clearly defining your vision for your marriage, you prepare to unleash the New Man within—a strong, confident, and purposeful individual rising to his full potential.

Keeping Score:

Reflect on the moments when you've felt frustrated, angry, or caught up in thoughts about your wife's failure to reciprocate your love. This is often when scorekeeping comes into play, cataloging your good deeds against her faults. This tally becomes your arsenal during disagreements, fueling conflicts rather than resolving them. Transforming from a scorekeeper to a leader involves changing how you perceive and handle these interactions. Referees don't win games.

Instead of keeping score, focus on developing your Lover's List. This powerful tool can help shift your perspective from tallying faults to recognizing and appreciating the positive aspects of your relationship. True leadership means setting an example, not just for yourself but also for your wife.

If you aim to lead your wife back to the fulfilling life you both envisioned, you must let go of negative scorekeeping. Embrace a leadership role that creates appreciation and gratitude, steering clear of resentment and blame. This shift is crucial for creating the marriage you both signed up for.

"If you want it, give it. Lead."

Bad Ass MoFo Statements:

The importance of affirmation statements for self-love, self-approval, and self-validation cannot be overstated. These statements are crucial for becoming the man who meets his own needs, energizes his life, and secures the Green Light in relationships. They are foundational for building a strong partnership in marriage.

We cannot exhibit the confidence necessary to thrive without belief in ourselves. If you're skeptical about the effectiveness of these statements, consider how negative self-talk has limited your progress and how you've often found yourself bitching over life or mindlessly scrolling through negative social media or conversations with negative friends.

I remember the first time I used one of these powerful affirmations. It was during a particularly low point when we lost our gym due to COVID-19. Starting a new program online while chasing the twins and pregnant with Riddick, Kathryn expressed fear, impacting me deeply. She said, "You'd be more manly if you were making more money."

This comment hit hard because I felt unappreciated despite my efforts to rebuild our lives. It wasn't as if I had lost our gym through mismanagement; the government had mandated its closure. We lost our income, home, vehicles, and most of our possessions. Her words felt like a direct attack on my manhood at a time when I was already vulnerable.

Initially, I reacted with anger and defensiveness, not recognizing where Kathryn's comment was coming from. Of course, our lack of financial stability fueled her fear. Instead of sitting in my pain, I chose to empower myself. Working exhaustively, trying to day-trade for a quick financial fix while managing endless work hours, I forged my first affirmation statement during this crisis. It was simple yet transformative:

"You are not less manly because you have no money. You are ALL manly because you work so hard to make money again."

This affirmation helped shift my mindset from fear and insecurity to strength and determination, reframing my perspective so I could start leading rather than reacting.

Now, it's your turn. Write down affirmations and place them where you'll see them every day—your office, bathroom, garage. Read them out loud, believe in them, and let them reshape your thinking. Speak the words into your heart. Despite initially doubting these affirmations and worrying about Kathryn's reaction, she eventually found them and found the exercise incredibly attractive, reinforcing the power of taking control over my narrative.

"Proof: you gain more approval by first approving of yourself."

Create one to three statements that address areas where you feel undermined or criticized. Use these affirmations not only to counteract negative thoughts but also to build your confidence and assert your role as a Man in Control, a Man in Power, and a Man with Impact. Remember, understanding the root of your wife's reactions—often fear—can help you connect more deeply and respond more effectively.

"Do not undermine your new skills; let your wife feel."

Affirmations like "I am strong" might seem over-simplified, but they are powerful reminders of your strengths and capabilities, especially in challenging times. Start crafting your statements now; affirm yourself, give yourself the validation you need, and remember: You're not just defending against criticism but building the foundation for a stronger, more resilient self.

"A Sexless Marriage: clinically defined as six months or more without sex. I define it to include Job Sex, Pity Sex, and Fear Sex. Then we can talk about No Sex."

Sex Mindset Shift:

You must shift your mindset around sex if you desire a truly fulfilling sex life in your marriage. It's the only way to avoid the truly unfulfilling sex life you are currently living. It's not just about physical satisfaction; true intimacy begins with understanding and connecting with your wife's mental and emotional needs. You may be unconsciously treating your wife as an object for sexual gratification, like a 'masturbation device' or a 'sex doll.'

"I hear robots are incredibly real these days, but Lords, we want more."

Reflecting on all levels of intimacy discussed in Man with Impact and thinking about the rejection ladder, remember that genuine intimacy is not limited to sex; it includes awesome conversations and shared experiences. If your wife feels used, she will withdraw, making her hesitant to engage in even basic affectionate acts like kissing or cuddling, fearing they might lead to unwanted sexual advances. Kathryn would scroll through dog rescues on social media just to avoid conversation. She didn't want it to go any further.

As a Man in Control, integrating respect and understanding into every interaction demonstrates that you value her beyond physical intimacy. This involves creating a safe environment using STAT Responses to handle her apprehensions, challenges, and even harsher confrontations when she runs into the side of your car. Through these actions, you're set to knock the wall between you, reigniting her passion and desire.

"This prepares you to be a Man at Play, where sex integrates mad passion again, rather than just a job for her to check off the to-do list."

Transformation of this stage may seem daunting and challenging, requiring you to effectively manage rejection as taught in Man with Impact and Man at Play. You must refocus your mindset from a selfish need to satisfy your urges to a partner-centered approach where your individual needs are equally considered. This adjustment helps ascend the rungs of the rejection ladder toward a fulfilling sex life that you both desire. Misplaced expectations and a sense of entitlement can crush your wife's libido; if she feels used, her desire will inevitably be depleted.

"Marriage is a partnership, not a power play."

You must challenge and eliminate any preconceived notions about sex, especially entitlement stemming from marital status or appeals to conveniently interpreted biblical passages demanding her submission. These expectations are misinterpreted and harmful, as they do not create mutual desire.

"Stop throwing the Bible at your wife. Biblically speaking, you're supposed to submit to her first."

You must understand that desire and arousal are distinctly different but equally important components of a healthy sexual relationship, as elaborated in Emily Nagoski's Come as You Ar*e*. This distinction is crucial; your wife's physical responses (like lubrication or physical arousal) do not always equate to a genuine desire for sexual engagement.

"Non-concordance: arousal does not equal desire."

7 TYPES OF SEX

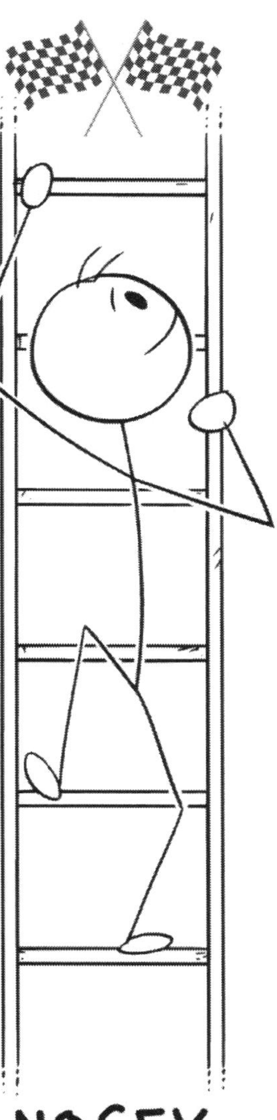

ANYTHING GOES – AS LONG AS SHE'S INTO IT. ACTIVITIES OR LOCATION ARE MUCH MORE EXCITING.

CRAZY SEX — SHE INITIATES

WHEN SHE DESIRES. SHE'S PASSIONATE AND WANTS MORE THAN A LITTLE. SHE WANTS TO EXPLORE.

CARNAL SEX — SHE INITIATES

SHE DESIRES, DESIRES TO DESIRE AND DESIRES TO CONNECT. SHE'S COMMITTED.

COMMITTED SEX — SHE INITIATES

SHE DESIRES TO CONNECT OR WANTS TO FEEL LIKE YOUR WOMAN. PERHAPS, TAKE CARE OF HER MAN.

QUICKIES — SHE INITIATES

IS SHE CHECKING IT OFF THE TO-DO LIST OR DOING IT TO SHUT YOU UP? "GET IT OVER WITH"

JOB OR PITY SEX — HEADED SEXLESS

IS SHE AFRAID OF YOUR MOOD, TEMPER OR ABUSE?

FEAR SEX — HEADED SEXLESS

SEXLESS MARRIAGE:
JOB SEX, PITY SEX, FEAR SEX AND 6 MONTHS OR MORE WITH NO SEX

NO SEX

The Seven Types of Sex:

Understanding the spectrum of desire in your wife is vital. Your wife's body can be good to go (arousal) but this does not equate to her heart and mind (desire) wanting to proceed. From spontaneous, passionate encounters that may happen at social events where your control and charisma attract her to more intentional 'commitment sex' where she might not be as spontaneously 'in' but still desires to connect with you. When you recognize these variations, you can manage expectations and gain a precious appreciation of your sexual relationship and her desire.

The Seven Types of Sex also include three detrimental types, leading to the eventual "No Sex." "Job Sex" or "Pity Sex," where the act becomes a task rather than a shared pleasure. At its worst, "Fear Sex" can occur, where sex is coerced through emotional manipulation or intimidation—an absolute sex life killer. Recognizing these dynamics are crucial for preventing them and ensuring she feel safe and valued. This is worth learning, as Kathryn will tell you:

"He destroyed me emotionally, and Fear Sex became our norm. Today, we have sex every day. I desire Cass, and I desire to connect with him."

Ultimately, the goal is to create a relationship where sex is a joyous and mutual activity, not a duty, obligation, or a source of contention. This requires consistent effort, understanding, and respect for your wife's feelings and needs. As you work through overcoming Job Sex and especially Fear Sex challenges, always strive to be a Man in Control and a Man with Impact, using the tools and techniques from The Reset to build a loving, respectful, and mad passionate marriage.

Addressing Job Sex is crucial for revitalizing your relationship. If your intimate life feels like a chore to your wife, it signals that fundamental changes are needed. Recognizing the nature of the sexual interaction you're having is the first step. Job Sex, where your wife feels obligated rather than engaged, can quickly destroy her desire and arousal, leading to avoidance of any intimacy. Her deeper dissatisfaction and disconnection are often signaled by common excuses, such as "I'm too tired" or "I'm not in the mood."

"At our worst, Kathryn would say, 'I think I'm asexual.' She believed it, too."

In the early years of my marriage, Kathryn often engaged in what we mistakenly assumed was Committed Sex but was actually Job Sex in disguise. She was trying to fulfill her perceived duties as a "good" wife. This kind of interaction might not be outright rejected, but it should be navigated with understanding and humor. Light-hearted comments like, "No babe, I'm hornier on Wednesdays," or "I can wait till you're ready, Baby," can help alleviate the pressure. While these won't solve the issue every time, they may encourage a more genuine engagement from her, potentially leading to committed sex, where she feels it's the right thing to do.

"Here, your wife will have a desire to desire or a desire to connect—until she desires. This is when she needs you."

It's essential to recognize when Job Sex is becoming a pattern. Preparing STAT Responses is crucial, especially when you start feeling neglected with your needs. Providing structure for your sexual relationship means moving beyond the frustration, anger, and the Nice Guy Triangle, all reducing your impact and making you appear as a victim—a Man without Power.

This dynamic can lead to Pity Sex, Fear Sex, or No Sex at all, pushing you further into a cycle of desperation where you're smothering your wife, seeking validation, and proving your worthiness, which is unattractive and ineffective, as you've learned.

"I love sex. I'm sure you do. Still, sex can never control you."

While sex makes you feel powerful, relying on it for emotional stability is unhealthy. Instead, strive to be a Man with Impact, focusing on emotional maturity and self-control. Avoid using sex as a weapon or a response to emotional triggers. If your wife initiates sexual intimacy, responding with rejection to mirror past grievances (especially out of spite or vindictiveness) does not display leadership or understanding. Instead, it reveals insecurity and a lack of control.

An important note: I teach men to expect less sex. Kathryn teaches women to expect much more. After thousands of couples through our programs, compromise is expected and generally skewed towards less than what you think you "need."

"You better get excellent at the things I teach if you want more sex."

Being Touched Out:

Dads don't really understand what it means to be "touched out." But you need to get it, and you need to get it quickly. She's a jungle gym for the kids. This is a common issue for mothers who spend extensive time physically engaged with their children, especially through breastfeeding or constant caregiving. When your wife is touched out, she must get the space she needs to recharge, and you need to respect this space and her physical boundaries.

Inappropriate gestures, even if playful, like squeezing or playful touches, can feel overwhelming. When you see her need for space and respect it, this is real care and consideration. This sets the stage for healthy and respectful interactions. Consequently, you can have the same adverse reaction to a gentle shoulder squeeze or affectionate hand on her back based on what she knows about you.

Forward Moving Mindset:

As you progress, remember your goal: sexual intimacy should be desired and enjoyable for you and your wife. An obligatory sex life is not loving or intimate. By shifting focus from merely fulfilling your needs to creating a loving, respectful, and engaging relationship, you pave the way for a healthier and more fulfilling sex life.

Man in Control is a man who understands, respects, and connects authentically with his wife's needs and emotions. In Man at Play, we'll create more excitement, fun, and the energy also needed in the relationship to complete your mad, passionate sex life.

Masturbation:

Masturbation is a sensitive topic that's entangled with misconceptions about male needs and marital intimacy. Orgasm and sexual release are natural. But no one is going to die if they go without it. Sex is not an essential daily requirement like food and water. Reframing your approach to masturbation involves understanding it's not merely about physical release but about cultivating a healthier sexual dynamic with your wife.

"You're wasting your time jerkin' off. That's time you could be using to get what you want."

Let's address the baseline: Masturbation, if you do it, must be free from harmful habits like porn use that damage the image of sex and intimacy. Understanding your own body respectfully and insightfully can be valuable, but this should be explored thoughtfully, perhaps as something to discuss in the future, following the guidance from resources like Destin Gerek's book, *The Evolved Masculine*.

Self-gratification fights against the objectives of a healthy marriage. Masturbation typically doesn't strengthen your bond with your wife, so a temporary shift away from it for at least a month can reframe your perception without harming your relationship. By committing to a 30 to 60-day period where you refrain from masturbation, you challenge the notion that sexual release is a survival necessity. This isn't just about proving you can go without; it's about recalibrating your expectations and focusing on enhancing intimacy with your wife.

"You won't want to touch yourself all the time when she wants to touch you all the time—do what that guy would do."

During this period, be mindful of how you manage life without masturbation. Many of you will be surprised when you do not die. You'll find that you will gain a clearer perspective on how to better relate to your wife. This is especially true regarding her feelings of guilt or inadequacy from your habits.

Ultimately, the goal is not to demonize masturbation but to understand it within the broader context of a fulfilling marriage. Once you've successfully navigated this initial period, it may be appropriate to reintroduce masturbation in a way that respects both your needs and those of your wife, aiming for a balance that contributes positively to your marriage. Most of you won't be ready for this kind of conversation for some time.

"With pornography, your wife will feel betrayed. And she more than likely knows you're using it. Connect the dots."

Time spent with pornography is taken from the time you could use to save your marriage. It's adding nothing to your positive emotional connection and distorting your ideas regarding sex. Focusing on setting the stage for the Green Light—a state where both of you are engaged and eager for intimacy.

The Checkered Flag represents the finish line where everyone is happy together! This journey is about enhancing your wife's emotional and physical connection, ensuring you are on track to a deeply satisfying, mad passionate relationship.

Providing Structure:

Making decisions is the cornerstone of providing structure in your marriage. If you can't decide effectively, steering your relationship becomes a challenge. However, decision-making gets easier with practice, particularly as you master STAT Responses and distance yourself from the Nice Guy Triangle. Mastery here doesn't imply infallibility—you might still make mistakes or change your mind. It's also perfectly fine to take deeper reflection before revisiting a decision.

The initial question to ask yourself is, "Am I in the Nice Guy Triangle?" Recognizing when you're trapped in this destructive cycle is crucial and challenging, so we offer additional training at https://MorrowMarriage.com/Tools. Decisions made within the triangle are often flawed, leading you off course.

The next step is to align your decisions with your core values to ensure that your choices propel you toward your desired direction. Once you are clear on these two things—getting out of the triangle and aligning with your values—MAKE THE DECISION. Stop saying, "I don't care," or "it doesn't matter." Even when a choice seems small or unimportant, it's crucial, as a man, that you take a stance in the direction you want to go - on everything.

"What would future you do?"

This skill becomes increasingly critical as we explore other roles, such as Man at Home and Man with Kids, and imperative as we move forward in the entire Passion Pillar. In these steps, you'll learn to impact your household, parenting, and life direction in ways that resonate with your core values, steering clear of the triangle. This is especially important if you're stepping up your involvement at home or navigating dynamics where your wife might be the primary breadwinner or decision-maker.

Your decisions will likely be met with resistance or accusations of manipulation. If you can't manage this effectively, it will be impossible to succeed as a Man at Play. I've witnessed many men struggle with this during coaching calls. They attempt to engage playfully but fail under their wife's rejection, leading to a loss of confidence and a resurgence of insecurities.

"BOOM! Back in the triangle."

Avoid the triangle, align with your core values, and confidently make decisions. This is how you reclaim control of your life and elevate your role within your family. Keep focused on who you want to be and watch the transformation in your family and life.

"Go out there, make those decisions, and Go Get Your Life."

Bonus Decisions:

Here's a bonus tip for those of you who hesitate in decision-making because you're seeking approval from your wife or avoiding her disapproval. Perhaps you dread a kiss because of the "gross" look she gives you, or you feel anxious talking to her due to her harsh criticisms. Maybe walking through your own front door or going on dates fills you with fear because you're constantly hiding or filtering your true self. You worry that any action might worsen the situation.

It's time to shift your perspective. When you make decisions aligned with your core values and outside the influence of the Nice Guy

Triangle, those decisions are right for you. Remember, your wife and family are integral to your values. Whether or not a decision directly benefits your wife, it remains consistent with your integrity and alignment. Embrace who you are. If you are making decisions from this place, there is nothing to fear. It's okay if your wife doesn't always approve.

"Agreement is not a prerequisite for respect and understanding in a relationship."

As you and your wife grow closer, you'll learn how to leverage each other's strengths in decision-making. But for now, focus on changing your mindset to one of confidence. Try this affirmation to start embedding this new mindset: "I am confident and can deliver my decision. Proud. Strong."

Embody this statement. Stand tall and be the Lord of your realm because you believe in the decisions you make. Express your opinions and state your preferences. Engage in activities that reflect your true desires. Be ready with your STAT Responses and handle reactions and rejections effectively. You will make impactful decisions and step into your role as a Man in Control.

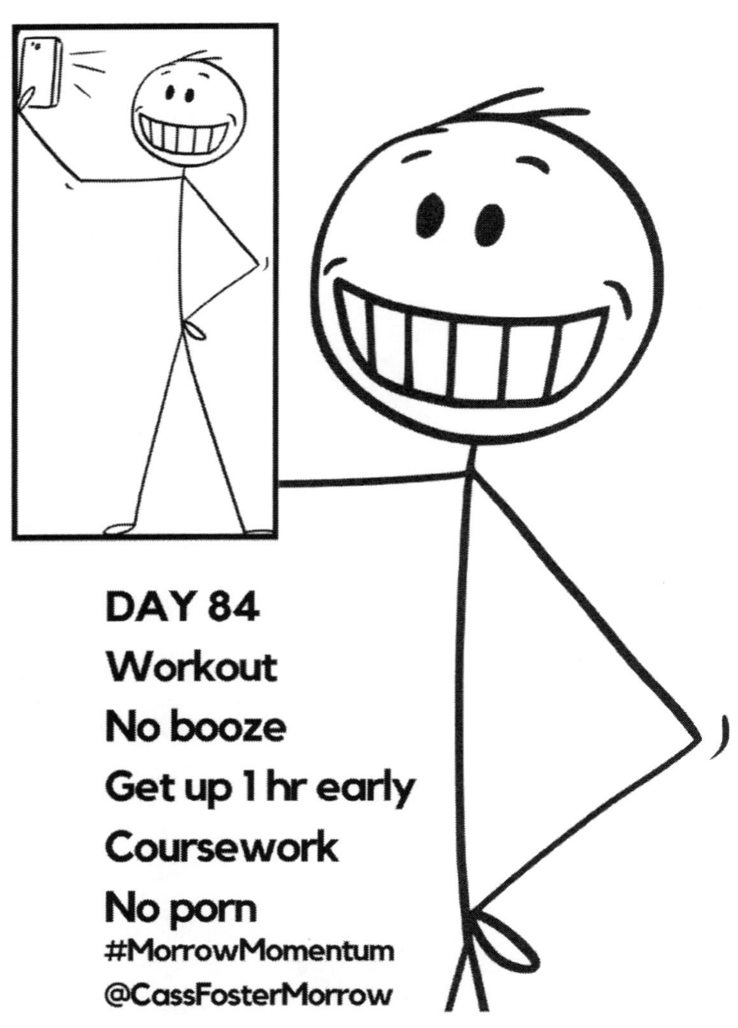
DAY 84
Workout
No booze
Get up 1 hr early
Coursework
No porn
#MorrowMomentum
@CassFosterMorrow

Your Comfort Zone Part II:

You might be tempted to skip this section, but I urge you not to. It is rapidly becoming recognized by Lords and random men and women joining me on my app, as one of the most effective ways to quickly transform your life —and they're only getting better at it.

Many men are deeply entrenched in their need for approval and validation from their wives. These men must discover who they are beyond their roles as husbands, fathers, professionals, hobbyists, and friends. Not using the program often results from deep, habitual patterns and coping behaviors that sabotage growth.

I've seen numerous men who make amazing changes at home fall into the comfort trap. They become complacent when they get what they want from their wives. This is also true for men whose wives coast along or disengage because they believe their husband's changes are temporary or insincere.

"You begin to slip backward."

Common responses from such wives include: "Why didn't you do this X years ago?" "How do I know this is real?" "I'm not going to fall for this again." and "How long will this last?" In more strained relationships—whether separated, in the process of divorce, or already divorced—wives might completely disengage by ignoring, blocking, or demanding more space, claiming "You don't respect my boundaries."

These challenges diminish your sense of empowerment and drive you to give up, playing the victim and ultimately quitting the program. I've developed a method to capitalize on your current momentum and to combat your desire to quit when you are in a low. This is a crucial part of The Reset and involves specific steps designed to push you out of your comfort zone and compel you to engage in hard conversations, helping you and your wife to grow rapidly.

What You Can Expect Through Morrow Momentum:

1. Accountability: Train yourself to be accountable to your standards, not just those around you. Stop paying for accountability and create discipline.

2. Pushing Limits: Deliberately push the limits of your comfort zone to create growth and resilience.

3. Handling Conversations: Engage in challenging dialogues as others—your wife and peers—become aware of your changes and the principles of the Reset.

4. Shedding Guilt and Shame: Learn to be proud of your personal growth and overcome the fear of disapproval.

5. Filling Your Cup: Learn how to self-nourish by giving and blocking out negative influences.

6. Inspiring, leading, and aiding in impactful, radical change in your partner, your children, people in your world, and the world beyond.

To ensure you're fully equipped to navigate these steps, I highly recommend accessing the in-depth explanations and live coaching sessions available from the initial launch of Morrow Momentum at https://MorrowMarriage.com/Tools. We also offer a free coaching call weekly for Momentum that is available on my app. The tools you can develop during these sessions will fill the gaps and provide you with a fully equipped readiness. While this book outlines what you must do, those resources provide a deeper understanding and practical guidance to help you implement these steps effectively and witness radical changes within weeks. Follow these instructions diligently; your commitment to this process is crucial for achieving the transformation you seek.

Brian's Journey with Morrow Momentum: A Case Study:

Brian participated in Morrow Momentum for 22 days when he experienced his first significant life change that resulted in his criminal charges being dropped. His commitment is a powerful example of how transformation can unfold through structured and supported self-improvement. Here's how you can replicate Brian's success:

Step 1: Commit to Daily Changes
On Day 1, initiate a daily routine that involves:

1. **Subtracting**: Remove one detrimental habit from your life. Common examples include excessive alcohol consumption or reliance on pornography, as was Brian's courageous admission.
2. **Adding**: Introduce a positive activity, such as dedicating 30 minutes to reading or coursework that supports your personal growth.

Step 2: Go Public
Public accountability plays a crucial role in maintaining your momentum:

- **Social Media Engagement**: Create and link social media accounts if you have not already. Instructional support, free coaching, ideas and examples can be found through Https://MorrowMarriage.com/Tools.
- **Daily Posts**: Document your journey on platforms like Instagram and Facebook. Post daily selfies, marking your progress with tags like: #Morrow Momentum and #DisruptingDivorce.
Mention or tag me: @CassFosterMorrow

Each post should highlight what you've subtracted and added while promoting transparency and accountability.

AND INCLUDE YOUR DAY COUNT: DAY 1, DAY 2, DAY 3…

"We've seen tremendous results on day 1 and repeatedly throughout the 60 days. Imagine day 562…"

Step 3: Engage with Your Community

· **Interact**: As you receive comments or messages, engage openly. Share why you've decided to make these changes and how the new activities benefit you.
· **Follow and Support**: Follow @CassFosterMorrow on Instagram and the 'Cass Morrow - Morrow Marriage' page on Facebook to stay connected with the community. They will lift you.

Step 4: Reflect and Respond

· **Daily Reflections**: With each new day, update your day count, reflect on your journey, and prepare for the next steps.
· **Manage Feedback**: Handle any negative feedback with STAT Responses, being mindful that tone can often be misinterpreted in text.

Step 5: Expand Your Impact
As you progress, consider how your changes can inspire and support others:

· **Community Contributions**: Consider extending the influence of your journey to others who might benefit, such as mentoring young men in juvenile detention or men in prisons, supporting military personnel, or integrating spiritual leadership into your endeavors.

"The incredible gifts to the world that men and women have given, partnering with us, has been insurmountable."

#MorrowMomentum: Harnessing Transformation

Morrow Momentum isn't just a challenge; it's a transformative journey that reshapes how you interact with the world around you. When you join Momentum, you take concrete steps toward self-transformation while inspiring others with your journey. By engaging in Morrow Momentum, you will conquer your Nice Guy and revolutionize your life.

"This was the missing piece to my program, The Reset, and the most effective tool for any struggling Nice Guy."

You Need to Share Your Transformation:

When you document and share daily progress, your narrative of change will inspire others and serve as a history of your transformation. It will set the stage for your evolution and encourage others to embark on their own journeys.

Break and Build Habits:

Morrow Momentum challenges you to subtract detrimental habits and add beneficial ones. This practice is the foundation for breaking free from old ways while creating new routines that empower you. It's about making incremental improvements that compound over time, leading to significant life changes. Simply, it's a method of adding and subtracting that aligns with your vision and core values.

Discipline and Growth:

A structured daily routine cultivates discipline that reaches into every avenue of life. This discipline produces growth, mental strength, focus, and the ability to keep your goals and values in sight even when challenges arise, and they will.

Purpose and Accountability:

This program is so successful because it helps you focus on yourself and your growth rather than your marriage issues or the chaos of life. It clarifies this process by teaching you to set daily goals and be mindful of your progress. This all culminates in a circle of accountability that flows from your core values and vision for life.

Insight into Your Core Values:

As you progress through Morrow Momentum, you'll gain deeper insights into what truly matters to you—your vision, purpose, values, and WHY you want to do this.

These insights empower you to "Go get your life!" with renewed direction and clarity. They enable you to make the right decisions, no matter who approves. You no longer need validation from others.

"We all have a wife, a job, and children. Make the impact you are born to make."

#MorrowMomentum is more than a self-help tactic; it's a foundational tool and system that equips you to take control of your life, embrace change, and pursue a path that leads to genuine fulfillment and joy. By committing to this process, you set yourself up for a life where your actions and values align perfectly, paving the way for lasting impact and personal mastery.

MAN AT HOME

Guard the castle.

Man at Home

As a Man in Control, you make clear and decisive choices while dropping your expectations by using Morrow Momentum and being a Man in Control. We'll dive much deeper into this in Man with Purpose, but it's time to bring your newfound impact into the home. In this phase of the program, we focus on transforming the dynamics of your marriage by creating a synergistic environment.

Many wives dream of a fairytale life. You might be a mad producer as a provider, but this alone doesn't fulfill your marital duties. As you now know, simply providing the "kingdom" doesn't meet all the emotional needs of your relationship. So, the gap between being Prince Charming and a provider can be massive in your wife's mind.

The concept of Prince Charming will be explored in depth in Man at Play as we discuss becoming a Lover, a Player, and a Magnet. However, there's more to address between the roles of provider and romantic partner, which we tackle in Man at Home and Man with Kids.

"If you live paycheck to paycheck or not getting ahead, you are not a provider, but you think you are. Regardless, providers, in general, need to listen up."

Many couples end up feeling like business partners or glorified roommates. This setup might create a stable foundation for managing day-to-day life, deceivingly suggesting that all is well. However, if intimacy is missing, it signifies a crucial gap—a wall between you and your wife. Even if you get along well and manage life effectively together, there's room for improvement, especially considering how "The Reset" principles integrate into the Partnership Pillar.

"Being a great roommate, business partner, or girlfriend with a penis will lead to coasting, settling, cheating, or divorce."

Being a Man at Home means more than just managing schedules or maintaining a household calendar. It requires a deeper and more authentic engagement. It's common for your wife to feel taken advantage of in this setup, leading to resentment and bitterness. During your transition, you might feel like her dad or her butler, as she might check out of her responsibilities. Recognize, in most homes, your wife has felt like she's become your mom or maid, a sentiment frequently echoed by women on my social media and in Kathryn's White Picket Fence Project. They express feeling like they have another child, not a partner.

Regardless of whether you're the sole breadwinner or if your wife stays at home, remember, you're both adults. Home care responsibilities don't disappear if she leaves; you'd still need to manage both work and home duties. Involvement as a husband is crucial. Take on household chores because you want to, not because your wife asked you to help. Engaging in this manner improves your living situation. It enhances the respect and affection between you and your wife, moving you both away from the roles of roommates or business partners towards a more loving and dynamic marriage—a team.

"In most 'Provider' cases, his job ends after his regular day, while mothers continue 24/7, and it's like Groundhog Day."

Getting Involved:

Taking the initial steps to become a Man at Home involves forging a synergistic partnership, a task that can initially feel daunting.

Particularly for those of you whose wives are stay-at-home moms or wives, this shift in dynamics might seem unnecessary at first glance. You might believe that if you effectively fulfill your traditional roles—yours being the provider and hers being the home caretaker— all should be well. However, this division of labor often undermines the intimate, foundational connection crucial to sustaining the safe Peace Pillar in your relationship.

Despite their practicality, such arrangements can lead to resentment. Your wife's day might be filled with endless tasks: managing the household, addressing the children's needs, and repeatedly tidying up. If she also cleans up after you, she may feel more like a caregiver than a wife. The maternal dynamic this creates is profoundly unromantic.

"No mom is sleeping with her child."

By stepping up this way, you alleviate some of her burdens and shift the dynamic from mother to equal. This shift is crucial for rekindling the intimacy and partnership that likely drew you together initially. Engaging more deeply at home sets a powerful example for your children, strengthens your relationship, and rebuilds the respect and affection that a lopsided division of labor might have eroded.

Step One: Look Around:

The first step in becoming a Man at Home is simply to observe—look around your living space with a thorough eye. As you engage more deeply at home, scan each room you enter—much like a police officer assessing a scene. This isn't about surveillance but about proactively identifying what needs to be done and taking action.

This practice isn't about the grand gestures you'll make; it's about recognizing the everyday tasks and nuances of maintaining your home. When you walk through the door, resist the urge to collapse on the couch as if your day is done. Your wife has been managing chaos all day, especially if you have kids, and the work isn't finished just because you're tired.

Start by noticing the small but significant things that need attention. Maybe there's a vacuum in the middle of the room or a diaper thrown near, but not in, the trash. These are opportunities for you to step in and help without being asked. If you see dishes piled up, put them into the dishwasher. Notice a laundry basket overflowing with clothes? Sort it out or start a load. Crumbs on the floor? Sweep them up before they're tracked all over the house.

Noticing also extends to home maintenance. You know that squeaky door you've been ignoring? Grab some WD-40 and address it. The cupboard door hinges are loosening; pick up a screwdriver. The toilet seat is loose. You know what to do. Even the least handy of men need to learn some basic freaking skills. These are not just chores. They are contributions to a well-run home. A functional household has members who are integral to its operation, not just guests who are waited on hand and foot.

Consider the personal hygiene and cleanliness habits that affect your shared spaces. Leaving a dirty toilet after use is not just discourteous—it's disrespectful. If you wouldn't leave a mess for a guest to encounter, why would you leave one for your wife? Start treating the cleanliness of your home as a reflection of your respect for the people you live with.

"It blows me away how many men blow up the toilet bowl and expect their wives to clean up the aftermath."

Being more observant and proactive in your home life isn't about keeping score or doing chores as a transactional act—it's about building a partnership where both parties feel supported and valued. By looking around and taking the initiative, you're not just cleaning a house but building a home. This sets a powerful example as you continue to engage as a Man at Home while smoothing the path as you explore deeper aspects of partnership in "Man with Kids" and "Man at Play."

"I don't really care if you do the 'outside' work. It's not like she's sitting around doing nothing while you're out there."

Step Two: Mirroring Your Wife:

The second step in becoming a Man at Home involves a thoughtful and observant approach known as mirroring. This doesn't mean mimicking your wife in a trivial or mocking way. It means genuinely paying attention to her routines and preferences so that you can align your contributions accordingly.

"As of now, this is her house. Do it her way."

Start by observing your wife's daily rhythms and chores. Notice when she does the laundry, how often she checks the pantry for groceries, or when she plans meals. If she regularly orders groceries, take the initiative—look in the cabinets and fridge, then ask yourself does anything need to be added to the shopping list? Better yet, if you can just do the shopping yourself. You also eat, and it's not her place to feed you or your family, even if you collectively decided that initially. That role (really) belongs to both of you. Doing this can significantly reduce her stress if she's been mothering you.

If your wife does certain tasks in a particular order, follow her lead. For example, she may start the dishes before vacuuming. Mirroring the process maintains routine without causing disruptions that could cause her to ram into the side of your car over minor issues. When you do this, you are learning how she manages her responsibilities, giving her respect in the process, and showing her that you can work within her systems effectively.

Another powerful aspect of mirroring involves taking on tasks that your wife dislikes. For example, if she dislikes folding laundry after washing it, you can handle it. This gesture shows empathy and understanding—it's about recognizing the small things that could make a big difference in her day.

Take on some tasks that are less obvious or often not appreciated. For instance, fill the car with gas or take on some home maintenance like cleaning the fridge or the dryer vent. Doing this, especially during challenging times, will lighten her physical and, most of all, her mental load.

"I don't particularly care for the chickens. We have them because they bring the family joy. If it's pouring rain, I will run out and put her pet chickens away for the night. Her exact words, the last time I did this: 'I love it when you do man jobs like keeping me out of the rain.' This really isn't rocket science, guys."

You're more than just helping out; you are a partner who follows through with respect, love, appreciation, and true support. You will feel supported in this environment as your home life becomes more balanced and engaging.

"I tell you to be more involved. Kathryn tells women to stop worrying if they are 'helping.' For now, go with what your wife needs."

Making Decisions:

As a Man in Home, it is important to extend your assertiveness into your decision-making. This means that you are actively leading, not just participating, in the daily operations of your home. You must master this process because every decision affects your daily life and your relationship with your wife.

Rather than defaulting to your wife's dinner suggestions, assert your preferences. If she suggests chicken or pasta, and you're craving steak, say it. This example illustrates that you are not confined to options presented by others but have an opinion based on your desires, and you express them.

Consider doing things with the kids. If you're passionate about football but your kids can't play because of health risks, find something else. Research and suggest alternatives that align with your vision for your family. In this way, you are actively shaping the direction of your family while also being very present.

Another area that many men let their wives take the lead is scheduling. The family calendar can be hectic. Planning dates, managing daily routines, or even deciding on home improvements require you to step in and contribute by making decisions. If your wife wants to remodel the kitchen, do the work and take the initiative to review the budget and discuss the possibilities. This doesn't mean taking control; it means sharing the responsibility and making informed decisions together.

Be prepared to handle disagreements or disapproval on this journey. Making decisions that align with your core values—even if initially met with resistance—strengthens the partnership by distributing the mental load and decision-making power more equitably.

"She's likely to challenge you since you have not been involved. She may even feel you're trying to control her."

An important aspect of decision-making is follow-through. If you commit to a task, complete it. Failing to follow through on commitments like fixing the garbage disposal or not hiring help when needed erodes trust and respect. Being consistent in your actions and accountable for your commitments will demonstrate you are reliable and trustworthy.

"Years ago, I had a client whose wife wanted the garbage disposal changed for four years. Don't be that guy."

Create and employ systems that support your decision-making and communication. If you aren't available due to meetings, make sure your wife has a plan to get in touch with you in case of an emergency. Something as simple as telling her to call twice in a row establishes clarity on handling this.

Take ownership of tasks around the house and forget about traditional gender roles. If you notice the car needs a wash or the fridge has had a tornado run through it, take care of it. Demonstrating pride in your possessions and attentiveness to the needs of your household without being prompted shows a commitment to shared responsibilities and respect for your shared environment. A man who handles his domain is a man who is worthy of following.

Enhancing your decision-making skills and integrating these principles into your life will strengthen your role as a Man at Home and create a deeper, more respectful partnership with your wife.

The Lover at Home:

Being a Lover at home goes hand-in-hand with a connected Partnership. In Man at Play, we will cover the Lover in-depth, but considering a partnership, let's look at listening differently.

Beyond romance, it's about creating a deep, attentive, and engaged partnership. This goes beyond simple conversation. It requires a fundamental shift in how you interact daily. You need to be present and learn to intentionally listen. It's easy to fall into the trap of monopolizing conversations with details of your day or problems at work, which often makes your wife feel sidelined. Your goal should be to ensure your wife feels heard and valued, not a wallflower for your soapbox or a punching bag from your stress.

"You're beating her heart, not her head."

Transform how you engage by making a conscious effort to listen more than you speak. Two ears and one mouth-use them in that proportion. When she shares her day and feelings, resist the urge to immediately relate it back to yourself. Focus on what she's saying and focus on what she is expressing. Ask questions that help uncover her deeper thoughts and feelings. Be curious and show genuine interest in her and her well-being.

"Stop piggybacking off of what your wife says just to talk about yourself."

Eliminate any distractions by turning off the TV and putting your phone away. Give her your undivided attention. If you're busy or focused on something like work or driving, acknowledge the importance of her words and suggest a time when you can be attentive and present. She deserves this type of focused attention. She deserves this (basic) level of intimacy.

You can implement active listening techniques by summarizing her points or clarifying her statements to ensure you've understood her correctly. This shows that you are listening and that you care to understand. Make mental or physical notes about topics she brings up. Things she feels passionate about or has deep concerns about should be topics for future conversations. When you do this, it shows her that you remember and value her thoughts and interests. By providing this kind of attention, you demonstrate commitment to her.

"You should be able to ask a question about something she spoke about a day, a week, a month later."

With this new approach, your wife may become distracted or even defensive. Just remain patient and use STAT responses to maintain control and direction. Doing this will improve your conversations and deepen your connection. Don't explain yourself; just use the tools at your disposal. Don't worry; with the right support, you'll become a master at these STAT Responses.

You must lead by example when it comes to minimizing distractions. If phone use is a problem in your home, be the first to put yours down and stick to it. Show through your actions that your time together is a priority; don't just tell everyone about your priorities.

Don't forget that this isn't just about your wife; it's also about you. This level of attention enriches your marriage and every aspect of your life. You will become an ally in your wife's eyes, not just a partner, but a trusted friend. You'll be someone she will want to share her deepest secrets with. Being a Lover at home is truly about building a relationship where both of you feel seen, heard, and deeply connected.

Navigating Common Struggles in Marriage:

Many men encounter typical struggles in their relationships, especially after years of their wives handling the majority of domestic responsibilities. This can often lead to a woman reinforcing her feelings of undervalue, as she's been relegated to the roles of mom and maid.

When she starts asserting herself, perhaps adopting an "It's my turn" attitude, it can seem like she's taking advantage or even being spiteful. However, this is rarely about taking advantage; it's more about "being allowed or able" to accept that "she matters." She might start spending more time on self-care, engaging in social media, relaxing, or pursuing her own interests—activities she may have put aside for years.

This shift may appear spiteful or vindictive, especially if she leaves the house a bit messy or starts leaving the kids with you more often. The key here is not to interpret her actions as disrespectful or secretive but to understand them as her embracing newfound freedom.

Your role isn't to control or resent these changes but to create a supportive, exciting, and adventurous environment—what I call the "Green Light" in your home. This means allowing her the space to explore and express her needs and desires unapologetically.

"Many men will find she completely 'Disrespects' as she begins to go out more now, acting single and free."

Incorporating strategies from Morrow Momentum and the Man with Purpose framework will equip you to mitigate any adverse reactions so you can support your wife's journey toward positive personal fulfillment. This is where you need to "Take the Oscar home." Consider this a mindset hack: think from her perspective by acknowledging that it might indeed be "her turn."

Even if it sometimes makes you feel more like her dad or a butler, don't forget that she had these same feelings toward you for a long time. Use the Patience Formula. Embracing this shift can transform your relationship into what I term a "Superpower Couple." When others see your dynamic, they won't just admire it; they'll aspire to it because it's genuine and fulfilling.

"They will WANT what you have."

If your wife was dead set on being a mom and wife, this would all sound irrational to you. After all, these were her goals. You made a plan together. Recognize that she put a ceiling on her life, dreams, and personal goals. In her sacrifice and loss of true partnership, many women will eventually gravitate toward creating a new life and raising their roof.

If you're aiming for a 'new' marriage, pushing through these initial challenges is crucial. Don't let frustration, insecurity, anxiety, or fear dominate your reactions. Act like you just got laid—adopt a relaxed, confident demeanor. This isn't just about getting through the day; it's about building a thriving, supportive partnership where both of you can shine. This is your next level, your new normal. Embrace it.

MANWITHKIDS

Slay the dragons.

Man with Kids

In Man with Kids, we will rev up the engine and slam the pedal to the floor. It's time to drive the Partnership Pillar home through teamwork and leadership, breaking from societal norms and our upbringing. Here, the challenges may be tougher than those in Man at Home, primarily because you might not have been as involved with your kids as needed, allowing your wife to set the pace for much more of this race.

Your wife is naturally loving, nurturing, and protective. She has established her rhythm in managing the children's needs. When you step in with intention and want to change the pace, be prepared for resistance. This is where your readiness with STAT Responses becomes critical.

Remember: your wife is not a single parent, and you're not just a provider. If your wife leaves you, you will still be responsible for your home and, most importantly, your children. This isn't about how much you earn or the material things you provide. No, it's about your legacy and your role as a father. You should want to rise up and become the best father you can be.

"Although uncommon, some of my Lords are faced with a dire need for support as, unfortunately, many women will begin to check out from their kids during this phase. I assure you this is equally unattractive for Lords. Reach out for extra help to lead her away from this type of freedom: https://MorrowMarriage.com/Tools."

Before reading this, many of you will excel beyond even my own efforts as a father. When the twins were about three months old, Kathryn told me, "You know, you need to love them too." I dove right in, and I have not looked back. Since then, I've dedicated myself to growth—constant reading and working with parenting coaches. I'll share some of these invaluable lessons here and in the list of resources at the end of this book.

In this chapter, I will summarize key insights to help you immediately and positively impact your family dynamics. This shift might surprise your wife if you've been less involved with your kids. Take the Oscar home and bring the energy of a puppy. It's infectious and can completely change the atmosphere in your home. We'll explore practical examples later.

However, paying bills, discipline, and occasional roughhousing with your kids does not make you a great dad. Most of you don't even follow through beyond the basic normal here. Avoid the trap of your own Groundhog Day—doing chores, taking on the kids, and expecting praise as if they're special tasks. Your wife has likely repeated these tasks countless times without acknowledgment. Imagine that monotony and think about how stifling it would be.

"Then, when you make promises to your wife about the kids, worse, to your kids, you don't always follow through."

Beware of the Nice Guy Syndrome. This can subtly manipulate interactions with your children. When my children prefer Kathryn's comfort over mine, it hurts my Nice Guy. Leaving this desire for validation unchecked will undermine your authenticity and damage your relationship with your kids.

Recognize these differences between your authentic self and your Nice Guy. You need to be able to identify this "guy" immediately when he shows up. Regarding your kids, it's crucial to STAT Respond with empathy, curiosity, and adventure rather than covert contracts. Love your kids without any expectation of how they will behave toward you. We'll talk about limits later.

Ultimately, when you take leadership and change your behaviors, you will strengthen your role at home. This approach reconnects you with your kids and reinforces your partnership with your wife, letting you collectively raise the Partnership Pillar. Let's shift gears and win this race.

"Although Dr. Glover coined the term 'Nice Guy' because he was talking about himself and the men he worked with, I believe it's our responsibility to break all patterns WE, as parents, use to create 'Nice Guys' AND 'Nice Girls.'"

The Team:

This chapter echoes the themes discussed in Man at Home, focusing on integration into your daily family interactions. Let's take a quiz: How attentive are you to the small details? How often do you step over your children's toys instead of picking them up? Do you change the bed sheets or tidy up without your phone in your hand? How proactive are you in managing daily tasks that support your family, like preparing snacks or packing the diaper bag? When was the last time you made a doctor's appointment for the kids or even gone? These aren't just chores but opportunities to demonstrate leadership and partnership.

"When you see something that needs to be done, just do it."

You're not cleaning up after your family; you're actively participating in your home life. This might feel like being a butler, but it's about more than just doing chores—it's about being involved and present, not just "there." Despite having a tight schedule and working much more than Kathryn, I prioritize helping her with the kids. It made a significant difference in her day and improved everyone else's day.

Making these minor adjustments shows you're a committed part of the team.

"Kathryn agrees; I am 'helping' because of our partnership dynamic now."

Your role as a father isn't just about providing but also setting an example. Whether your behavior is exemplary or poor, your children are watching and will emulate you. Teach them about responsibility, integrity, and teamwork by being a teammate rather than a taskmaster. DO, don't DICTATE! If your teenage children lack respect for you, it might be because they're reflecting the example you've set. Take a look in the mirror to find out.

Think about the Nice Guy Triangle. Do you want your children to replicate your relationship behaviors? Is this thought unsettling? Knowing how my life played out, it's a scene from a horror movie. By learning from me and transforming your approach to marriage, you will disrupt negative patterns and stop them from being passed down to your kids.

"Not one man gets on a call and doesn't have his kids in mind."

Consistency is the key to instilling values of reliability and integrity in your children. As they see you live out your core values, they'll learn to apply them and recognize the impact of the legacy you're building by going through Morrow Momentum. Then, after a sporting event, for example, engage them in making decisions like choosing between ice cream or pizza instead of "I don't know" or "I don't care." This teaches them to participate actively in family decisions yet live a fulfilling life beyond the norm.

For example, be present by reducing screen time and engaging more directly with your children. They will feel neglected if they need help to capture your attention because you're often distracted by your phone. You may have already been pushing the screens on them or allowing them for too long. You have some work to do. Being present—making eye contact and actively listening—shows them they are valued. Follow through on your commitments. Take them to the park or that special event, as promised.

The foundation you build for your children to learn responsibility and integrity is directly related to your involvement and authenticity. You are teaching them every day through your actions and values. Consistently being present and fulfilling your promises to yourself and them, will model the importance of reliability and commitment. This sets the stage for a legacy of strong, positive leadership within the family.

"Your kids should be your reason; don't make them your excuse, and don't excuse yourself because you don't act as though they are your reason."

Love Your Kids Through It: Embracing Emotional Connection:

Allow your children to express their emotions fully and safely. This is similar to how you interact with your wife but tailored to your children's needs. They require more time for empathy and validation, which helps them understand and articulate their deeper feelings. By responding with STAT Responses, you teach them effective communication that will benefit their future relationships.

"It's imperative that you do not rush past Triggers, as your children require more help in this area."

Our children often seem like little narcissists, but they are certainly not. Children are naturally selfish; their perception of the world centers around their needs and experiences. When kids exhibit strong reactions or emotional flip-flops, even gaslighting you, it's not a manipulation but a struggle with emotional regulation.

"Crazy when that light bulb clicks."

Telling a child to "Stop screaming" or "Don't cry" dismisses their feelings. Try acknowledging their emotions by saying, "You are really thirsty. That's hard. I'll get you the water, but I need a minute." This helps them feel heard, even if their immediate reaction is disbelief.

Remembering the example from earlier is imperative. Parents have had this entirely wrong. When a child tells you, "I can't go to sleep; there are monsters in the closet." Your child tells you, "I am scared I won't see you tomorrow. I didn't spend enough time with you today. I feel alone and need you." When our parents dismissed our fear, we did not learn how to understand what we were feeling. When, out of frustration or a need for a break, we tell our kids to go to sleep, we do the same. Our children will grow up as we did, unable to share their true feelings.

"Yet, men and women are expected to know how to communicate in a marriage."

Bedtime presents common examples. Consider a night when Vale was upset because she wanted to wear her new pajamas. Our instinct might be to react defensively (SAFE React), feeling inadequate or rushed. What's required is not a solution to the pajama issue but a recognition of her need for connection. She's not just upset about pajamas; she feels the impending disconnection when bedtime means you're not around.

In these moments, talking less and being present with empathy is crucial. Children like Vale react strongly to the immediate situation because it triggers deeper fears of disconnection or abandonment. These reactions are intense and also opportunities for profound connection.

When they express their emotions like Briar, crying, screaming, and even biting, they seek reassurance of love, most of all.

"Our children have never been abandoned or seen nastiness between Kathryn and I. This should signify a need for rapid change in most homes."

From personal experience, I've learned that allowing our children to express themselves, even in their most intense moments, leads to quicker recovery and deeper bonds. Briar's biting was an extreme form of communication, and in my early parenting journey, I might have responded with anger or punishment, but now I understand the importance of staying calm and connected. Albeit difficult for Kathryn and me, this approach helps them calm down sooner and teaches them that it's safe to express their feelings.

As a parent, your job is not to stop or prevent emotions but to guide your children through them. Dads should be a stable presence that helps them navigate these scary feelings. This will help them identify what they actually need, and through STAT, you can show them how to communicate accordingly. As a dad, you'll face times when your patience and resolve will be tested. You'll remember that parenting is not easy, but by maintaining your composure and focusing on connection, rather than correction, they will see you as the leader they need.

I've said this many times: Consistency is your best friend; the key to success. Another reason Morrow Momentum was the missing piece to the Reset and The White Picket Fence Project. Keep the Green Light always on by showing you are a safe space for their emotions. This consistent, loving approach will help them at the moment and teach them how to handle emotions constructively as they grow into adults. This is part of your legacy—the emotional wisdom and resilience you instill in your children, which they will carry into all aspects of their lives.

"God knows the world needs leaders. Our children's world will need them more."

Praise and Punishment:

Our children mirror us. Yours will learn how to respond using STAT Responses, ensuring they don't hide their feelings—you can already show them how to share feelings correctly. We are steering clear of triggering SAFE reactions. Help them identify their needs within STAT. Focus on using curiosity so your children are encouraged to dig deeper into their feelings and needs.

"This focus helps prevent the development of 'Nice Guys' or 'Nice Girls. Damn, I'm proud of this."

My own experience as a Nice Guy was shaped early on. My parents set a course that took me decades to correct. Currently, my program's average age is 44—decades behind. I'm committed to ensuring our children don't fall into that same trap. In our approach to praise and punishment, we emphasize connection over correction, adopting what is known as 'connected parenting' with a few twists. This method helps children feel supported and understood rather than judged and molded by external expectations or the need for approval.

"Our children can still be held accountable through limits and natural consequences."

Praise:

We learned the concept of connected parenting through a lot of time and resources. Michelle Kenney, @peaceandparenting, coached us personally; what we learned from her was invaluable. I've implemented a great deal of this education in the creation of Man with Impact. You can find more about her and her company, Peace and Parenting, in the resources section at the end of this book. This approach helps us break the traditional cycle that often creates Nice Guys and Nice Girls who depend too heavily on parental approval and validation for their self-worth and identity.

In our home, we consciously allow our children to express their emotions freely, shifting away from relying solely on praise and punishment. This is a core concept within The Reset and now here. By changing how we handle these interactions, we're teaching our children to value their own feelings and achievements without constantly seeking our approval.

For example, instead of simply congratulating them for a job well done, we encourage them to reflect on their efforts by asking, "You worked really hard at that. How does that make you feel?" This helps them internalize their accomplishments and develop a sense of pride in their efforts. This doesn't mean you'll never say, "I'm proud of you" or "Great job," but you want to be mindful not to set them up for seeking your approval and validation.

"And the approval of their future husband or wife's."

When reinforcing these achievements, we focus on their internal growth rather than the external outcome. Saying things like, "Your hard work really paid off. I'm so proud of you. What did you learn from this experience?" encourages them to appreciate the process and their own developmental journey, not just the end result. This approach is tied to the principles we've established in The Reset, which aim to create independence and self-assurance rather than dependency on external validation.

We also work to ensure our children understand the concept of natural consequences, which goes hand-in-hand with learning responsibility, an essential part of avoiding the Nice Guy Syndrome. Instead of punitive measures that don't correlate with the behavior, we have conversations about logical outcomes, such as the natural discomfort of feeling cold if they choose not to wear a jacket.

"Common sense is learned; it's not taught."

By applying the skills you've learned from The Reset to our parenting methods, we're enhancing our children's ability to grow into well-rounded individuals and ensuring that they do not fall into the patterns of seeking constant approval or avoiding disapproval. This creates a space of healthy development where they can thrive and feel secure in who they are as they learn to understand and manage their own decisions and emotions.

Punishment:

Addressing the challenge of setting limits without creating the Nice Guy or Nice Girl Syndrome involves a nuanced approach that balances understanding with accountability. This isn't just about enforcing rules; it's about guiding our children through their feelings and actions in a way that creates independence and responsibility.

When it comes to discipline, it's crucial to avoid punishments that don't logically relate to their actions. For example, taking away their toys for not eating dinner doesn't make sense and won't teach them the importance of healthy eating habits. Instead, logical consequences—like discussing the importance of nutrition and setting expectations for mealtime behavior—help them understand the impact of their choices. "The kitchen is closed." would be an appropriate consequence if it's past the time to eat.

Consider the situation where your child has stayed out too late or has been caught drinking at a party. Instead of reacting with a knee-jerk punishment like grounding them for a month, which can create resentment and fear, a more effective approach would be to discuss the natural consequences of their actions. Talk about how they felt the next day, the potential legal issues, and the dangers associated with such behavior. This approach helps them understand the seriousness of their actions without feeling alienated from you.

As a disciplinarian, it's important to be more of a guide than an authority figure. When your children make mistakes, say, "I'm not happy about what happened, but I love you. Let's discuss it and figure out how to prevent this in the future." Doing this eliminates the shame and fear when we express anger or disappointment, creating a space where they feel safe to come to with their needs and problems. "I'm very angry, but I love you. Now, is it a good time to talk about X?"

This method also involves a significant shift in how you interact with your wife in these situations. Maintaining a united front is crucial even if she disagrees with your approach. You may need to have private discussions to align your parenting strategies but show support for each other in front of the children whenever possible. This unity is vital for creating a stable and secure environment for them.

Ultimately, your goal is to teach your children that every mistake is an opportunity to learn and grow. Instead of feeling ashamed or guilty, they should understand that it's okay to make mistakes as long as they take responsibility and learn from them. This approach helps them develop a healthy sense of self and prepares them to handle life's challenges with resilience and confidence.

By adopting this strategy, you avoid creating a cycle of fear and avoidance and instead build a relationship built on mutual respect, understanding, and personal growth. This way, you're not just raising obedient children out of fear but developing young individuals who respect themselves and their decisions and are equipped to face the world with confidence and integrity.

STAT and Breaking Our Children from The Nice Guy or Girl:

Connection with our children is fundamental to our current relationships and their development. Whether dealing with a toddler's explosive emotions or a teenager's rebellious, angry silence (or screams), the need to maintain a steady and understanding presence is crucial. This is where STAT Response becomes essential in our interactions, ensuring we meet their outbursts with calmness and control instead of mirroring their energy and attitude.

"Don't forget to bring in the adventure."

Our instinct might be to "fix" their issues, especially when their behavior triggers our Nice Guy tendencies, where we desire to smooth over problems quickly and keep everyone happy—or demand respect. Fixing the issues will deepen the disconnect because it doesn't address the underlying emotional needs. Instead, by maintaining our Green Light—a signal of safety and openness in the home—we encourage a healthier expression of emotions.

All of this plays a significant role in nurturing connection. If our kids are scared of our reactions or feel they must earn our approval to receive love, we inadvertently create a Red-Light atmosphere of fear and disconnection. By creating an environment where they feel safe to express their feelings and make mistakes, we reassure them of our love and their value in our eyes.

"It's possible to have 'one Peace Pillar up and one Peace Pillar down' with your wife and children. Also, you can have peace with one child and not another."

Setting Limits:

You need to set limits. Our children are still children, no matter their age. Setting limits is essential, but it's not just about enforcing rules—it's about guiding our children to responsibly manage their emotions and actions. When setting limits, it's important to note that we are often out of time or trying to keep our children safe. As a Man with

Purpose and someone striving to be a Man with Impact, it's crucial to understand that setting limits is part of teaching our children how to navigate the world safely and effectively.

When we set limits, we often default to running out of patience or control, but it's more about creating a safe environment where our children can explore their emotions within reasonable boundaries.

Here are a few examples. When a child complains of their distaste for the bath and the water in their eyes, a connected response would be, "That's tough. I don't like feeling water in my eyes either, but we need to get clean." This shows empathy while reinforcing a boundary, teaching them to manage disappointment. Now, they may provide a well-rehearsed tantrum, but it doesn't matter; you're going to allow them to feel. Before their next bath, remind them again about the importance of cleanliness.

Similarly, for toddlers acting like ninjas jumping from unsafe heights, we guide them by saying, "I know you want to jump off the couch. It's a lot of fun, but it's not safe. I can't let you do that." Riddick likes to throw things. I'm pretty sure he's going to break the TV soon. That's his new thing. He just throws everything he can find. Rather than freaking out and punishing him, I try to connect with him. I get down to his level, and I stop him. Holding him firmly, I say, "I can't let you throw things like that. It's OK to be angry. No matter how angry we are… we can't throw things." This works for hitting as well.

For teenagers, who might demand privacy or react sharply, maintaining connection is about respecting their need for space while still setting boundaries, "No matter what you're feeling, you can't treat me that way. I love you no matter what, though. I'm not going anywhere."

Conflicts between siblings, or when Riddick throws things, offer opportunities to teach rather than simply punish. Remember, instead of reacting angrily, connect with them at their level. That includes getting down on their level.

Bringing The Partnership Pillar Home:

In the context of The Reset and our roles as fathers, we are not just disciplinarians; we are leaders, teachers, and safe havens. Our goal is to embody the principles of The Reset, which means engaging our children during disciplinary moments and everyday interactions. Whether turning daily chores into a song or game or ensuring that our phone is away during dinner, these actions strengthen our connections.

Giving your wife a break from her duties by stepping in to handle the children demonstrates your commitment as a husband. This action not only supports your wife but also models the dynamics of a healthy and supportive relationship for your children. It's about showing that you can be a playful and present parent, which enriches the family dynamic and solidifies your role as a Man in Control who is capable of managing both the needs of your children and the expectations of your marriage.

Scheduling one-on-one 'dates' with your children—where you focus entirely on them without distractions—reinforces your connection and gives your partner (an often needed) a break. These moments build relationships with each child and show them they are valued and loved for who they are, not just for what they do or how well they behave. Never underestimate the power of this type of bond. If one thing will help a child become secure and confident and avoid being the Nice Guy, this is one of the best opportunities.

As you've cruised through up until now, these efforts build a family environment where each member feels understood and supported, capable of expressing themselves without fear of rejection or misunderstanding. This is your legacy as a father: to build a bedrock of trust and love that empowers your children to grow into confident and compassionate adults ready to handle whatever challenges life throws their way, especially marriage.

This is your legacy! Get this dialed in. If this is all new to one or both of you, you may still have some struggles with your wife; however, when she sees that your children are respecting you and talking to you differently, helping you, getting chores done, and having a fun and connected time, she is going to notice and come along for the ride.

Many wives initially get a little jealous and resentful toward Lords. That's okay. This is her running into the side of your car again, challenging you. You show up as a Man with Impact and love her through it. It's that simple. This is a major component of finalizing the Green Light and establishing your partnership. This lays the foundation for your leadership. In the next section, Man with Purpose, you will learn to become a leader in life. This will exemplify your Green Light. You will become valuable, yet you will still have time for your wife and family.

"People pay a lot of money for high value. How do you think your wife and children will treat you, the highly valuable New Man?"

The Passion Pillar

Passion

"This part of the book will feel very personal because it is. I'm going to write it more loosely. A little more freely. I want you to feel a little less anxious and lifted. I've got plans for you. We're about to ACTUALLY Go Get Your Life and Go Get Your Wife."

I've spent years of my life helping people transform their lives from the ground up, especially in the area of health and fitness. In my relationship, I moved from saving sexless marriages to 'leveling up' marriages. Once Kathryn joined me and shared in complete transparency, we moved to save 'bad' and toxic marriages. Now, Lords and I have moved from marriage to relationships and leading other men—to men, LEADING THE WORLD WITH ME.

"Watching 1000s of men move: If you only care about saving your marriage, instead of the impact you can make leading men, you will more than likely fail."

You must become valuable. A highly valuable man has more on the go than his job, wife, and kids. Relationships are valuable, and when you can show up using The Reset, you have abundant life to offer.

"You become invaluable."

I did not understand this fully until working with one of my mentors. Evan Carmichael, @evancarmichael, inspires coaches to become movement makers. As I transitioned into coaching, I witnessed

Kathryn's transition from adoration to complete awe with me. As Evan would say, it's time for you to 'believe.'

To put this in perspective for you, Kathryn is grateful for the money I make. She not only thanks me for working hard and when I pay for things, she also leads the children in showing gratitude towards me for it. However, when she thanks me for being her husband, expressing her awe and pride, it's because of the impact I'm making in the lives of others.

For example, when a testimonial comes in and I'm clearly responsible for helping someone, that's when she throws her arms around me to thank me. She'll sit on my lap, touch my face and tell me she's proud to be my wife. Not because of the money I make, but because she knows I saved someone no one else did. When you are invaluable, you are next level.

This is precisely why I'm warning you not to pick and choose what you want to implement. You must follow the whole system I have laid out. Man with Purpose and Momentum will get many of you out of your comfort zone, but its only scary until you've done it. The benefits far outweigh your fears.

MANWITHPURPOSE

Go Get Your Life.

Man with Purpose

"Before finding my purpose, I was wasting my life. I realized I was living in quiet desperation. Now, I'm leading in life. Having a purpose beyond my job stopped me from drowning and saved my life."—Dennis Emmitt, USA. Mentor To Lords.

Becoming a Man with Purpose and realizing your true potential impact on the world is one of my favorite sections of The Reset. I hate that most men are literally the same; they're boring. They only have their job, wife, and kids. If they have hobbies, those hobbies mean nothing. It might be for a bit of fun. You watch too much TV, scroll through social media too often, and are making no (real) progress in life outside of work. Purpose changes your trajectory.

"IMPACT CHANGES EVERYTHING."

Since we know why you're reading this, the first reason is that your wives will look at you differently when you have a purpose, and your purpose makes an impact. You're exciting to talk about because you have more things to talk about than just your job. You are somebody that she can talk about to others.

Then, when your wife listens to her friends, family, or whoever complains about her husband, you stand out positively. When we bring our true energy of who we are, how excited we are, how excited we are about our lives and our purposes, this solidifies your Green Light.

Man with Purpose is in the Passion Pillar because it is very attractive to your wife when you are a highly valuable man in extremely high demand. Yet you continue showing up as a Man (out of the triangle) at Home, with your Kids, and ready to Play. You're in total control, and your wife feels safe. You show up as her partner, even though you are so busy changing the world.

"You may not believe this yet or believe you need it. You will, and you do."

Your wife is going to want you, and we haven't even visited the fun stuff with Man at Play to amp up her desire and your seduction. None of this will be used to manipulate or make your wife feel jealous or insecure. There will be no toxic masculinity or glorified dating advice we discussed earlier. You are not doing this to create negative anxiety or to control your wife.

"I'm going to mentor you now, my style: DO NOT FUCK WITH ME with the Passion Pillar. This will define you as a Lord and leader in life. DO NOT abuse it."

Let's touch on the Lover, Player, and Magnet from Man at Play to lay the foundation of the Passion Pillar with Man with Purpose. We've covered many components of the Lover so far. We have also unknowingly introduced the Magnet throughout the book. The Magnet is all about creating polarity. It's the natural attraction that I will explain in Man at Play.

The Magnet can automatically attract your wife. This isn't the canned garbage you've seen or the stuff on nonsense social media feeds. This is about attraction for long-term sustainability in a marriage. When you are competitive and achieve status, yet continue to give more, this is attractive for your wife. In fact, it's attractive to the world. Look at how I have moved so fast in two short years. This also forces you to have ambition, drive, and focus. You are defined by your "Why," derived from your purposes and the impact you will make.

"When your why stands out, you stand out. When you stand out, your wife stands with you."

Even if your wife's not there yet, the people in her life will notice and point this out to her, making you stand out. Essentially, they begin to sell you. This is why we have been focusing on making social media posts, using day counts that add and subtract things guaranteed to move you toward success in your life. You must be focused on achieving and growing as a man. Remember, when you're a 10, your wife has to meet you.

This is where many of your wives will need you to lift them with your newfound energy and excitement from your purpose(s). When you bring purpose energy home, and it lifts the morale of the home, your wife can't help but notice your Green Light. This will motivate your wife to start doing the same types of things. This may not happen immediately, but as you stay consistent, it will become glorious.

When you are fulfilled with purpose, your wife will crave purpose. When you both have impact, you will thrive with this energy. This makes you the Superpower Couple as passion falls into place. This makes any man unstoppable. Embrace the opportunity here to compete with yourself. I'm about to show you how you will truly inspire your wife. At the bare minimum, we can create something that the Magnet needs to deliver to his wife: anticipation, uncertainty, and attention–positively.

"Straight up, you need to start working out and eating right."

Lords Transformation:

Assuming you did not put the book down and get started, the first addition to your Morrow Momentum Day Count should be committing to a fitness and proper nutrition regimen. Having worked with over 3,400 men by the time of writing this, I've seen that most men neglect their health. If you already work out, add it anyway, or use a gym selfie for your DAY count.

We are on a journey from dad bod to sex god. I ran a gym for 22 years before COVID hit, and we were forced to shut everything down. In marriage coaching, I initially hesitated to push fitness too hard for fear of pushing men away. Now, I see it's an integral piece. It's one of the quickest ways to make your wife notice you're serious about change. It's also a way to make you stand out against most people.

I'm 43 years old, and in the gym, I feel like a senior citizen—that's just crap. Let's get one thing straight: the dad bod isn't as attractive as some make it out to be. If your wife insists it is, it might be out of her insecurity, perhaps because she's not ready to step out of her comfort zone either. I'm not saying you need a six-pack, but muscles are hot. That's why women buy firefighter calendars and flock to shows like Thunder Down Under. It's why any Hollywood leading man worth his salt is ripped when he takes his shirt off. That's just reality.

Kathryn, for example, is incredibly confident yet perpetually dissatisfied with her body, regardless of how tight she is. Sometimes, she tells me she doesn't want me to have a six-pack, but whenever my veins are parallel to my underwear lines, she absolutely loves (one in particular). She might play it cool, but let me reiterate: muscles are hot. Lean is hot. You command respect and authority with your presence. When you're physically fit, people take you more seriously. Listen to Andy Elliot for an hour on his Instagram. The man won't even hire you if you're fat. It's about time someone talked about it seriously.

Muscles make people interested in listening to you, laugh at your jokes, and assume you know what you're talking about. It's a psychological thing. When you look like you've mastered your body, people assume you have mastery in other areas, too. You need to work out five, maybe even seven days a week. The more frequently you do it, the quicker you'll develop the habit and the more energy you'll have. That energy is crucial for bringing the Green Light into your home, playing with your kids, and building those essential connections.

"This is non-negotiable."

You must be committed to fitness if you want to work with me. You need to eat right, work out, and consider supplements. With my 22 years of experience in fitness, I'll break down everything you need to know about nutrition, fitness, and supplements. When I owned the gym, we charged $350 a month for group fitness classes three times a week, which was way above what others charged, but our program was unmatched. For years, I was all over the news and won several awards as the city's best personal trainer. While I'm not looking to return to that career, I know how crucial this knowledge is for you.

No jokes, no BS—you'll eat healthily, work out, and cut out alcohol. Alcohol impedes your fitness goals and hampers your ability to control your emotions and provide the necessary direction and structure at home. If you're still drinking, it's time to stop. Use this commitment to set an example for your wife, showing her you're serious about making changes.

You know you need to appear as a protector. You should be physically capable of protecting your family and playing with your kids, and you should be confident, with your chest out and your posture perfect. I won't list all the benefits of health here. Just know this: You are undergoing a Lord's transformation now, from dad bod to sex god. You don't need to look like a Spartan soldier, but you do need to take your health seriously. I will help you with this shortly.

Nutrition:

Let's dive into our award-winning nutrition plans. I'll explain why they're crucial and how to pick the right one for you. Initially, when we owned a gym, we hired Alex Hormozi, a guru in transforming gyms into highly profitable ventures. He now teaches people, for free, how to make millions of dollars. His book outlines his strategies, which is a must-read if you're aiming to start your own business. Alex helped us realize the potential of our gym, guiding us towards seven-figure earnings before the pandemic hit.

Before meeting Alex Hormozi, our approach to dieting was straightforward: here's your diet, now lose some weight. However, Alex introduced us to a novel concept—wrapping our plans into a 6-week challenge. This structure enabled our clients to see rapid results. Leveraging Kathryn's Master of Science in Nutrition, we crafted tailored plans suited to various weight goals, and they were highly effective.

Our focus is on quick, visible changes. The challenge diets are designed to produce rapid results, but for more rapid–we have a rapid fat loss plan. We offer a massive weight gain plan for those needing to bulk up, which works even without an intense weightlifting regimen. Start with a plan that resonates with you. These challenge diets are simple but ensure you're consuming the right macros to meet your goals.

Incorporating these diets with regular workouts, typically three times a week, men have lost between 24 and 32 pounds in just six weeks. That's a solid start, but remember, we'll tweak things after the first six weeks to continue your progression. For those in a hurry, the rapid fat loss program is your best bet, usable for up to 120 days, but remember, don't extend beyond this period. If you're on the Massive Weight Gain Program, it's an excellent beginning, and we can guide you further in Lords to ensure the weight you gain is muscle, not fat.

At this stage, the choice of workout or diet plan isn't critical—just choose one and stick to it. If your wife suggests pizza for dinner, remember your commitment. Even if your family wants pizza, stick to your meal plan. This showcases your integrity and control, proving you're the new man without talking about the new guy. Also, don't go for beer and wings with friends. Show leadership in all of your relationships.

We've also included hacks like a meal prep guide to simplify your week and potentially relieve any responsibility from your wife, affirming your commitment to your new health goals. If you're often dining out for business or date nights, use the restaurant ordering guide provided in our resources. This is a common discussion in Lord's coaching calls—how to maintain your diet in social settings.

"Whenever people eat healthily, they always think they deserve all sorts of cheat meals. They want nights off with drinks. But, whenever you're eating like crap or drinking, you don't say, "I want a 'healthy' cheat day."

Don't let a day of challenges or poor choices be an excuse. Use the meal plans as a shopping list with services like Instacart to make grocery shopping a breeze. We've even included a travel guide for maintaining your diet on business trips or vacations. Choose your plan, set a meal prep day, and start transforming. It's the fastest way to show you're serious—to yourself and those around you.

All Lord's Transformation Resources:

Nutrition, Fitness, Guides, and Supplements are available at https://MorrowMarraige.com/Tools. Plans for your wife are available through The White Picket Fence Project.

Fitness:

I'm handing over my award-winning workouts and best-selling of all time. You're welcome. When scheduling your workouts, choose any physical activity you enjoy. However, remember the mantra: muscles are hot. Nothing can substitute for adding muscle and shedding fat to enhance those muscles. Many of you may set goals like losing 20 pounds, but realistically, you might need to lose 40 and gain 20 in muscle to achieve the desired look.

While it's tempting to dive into activities like jiu-jitsu, yoga, or rock climbing—and yes, you can include these—lifting weights should be non-negotiable. I recommend lifting at least four times a week, preferably seven if you've struggled with consistency. The reason is simple: you must replace your old habits with new routines until they become ingrained. While there's a sustainability factor, the immediate goal is to kickstart your muscle growth, enhance your mobility, and boost your confidence and energy.

"Working out only three times a week covers less than half the week. How can you expect real or rapid results when you're not committed."

You're already on the right track with nutrition, so let's complement that with muscle growth. I offer workout plans ranging from one to three-and-a-half hours, tailored to different endurance and strength levels.

I've also crafted a wicked 90-day challenge adapted from Andy Frisella's renowned 75-hard program, which is intensely focused on building muscle. This pairs perfectly with the mental and lifestyle reset we're already tackling. For those who need quick results in toning and shaping, I have a series of HIIT (High-Intensity Interval Training) workouts that were so good that I didn't change the structure for over 13 years. These are effective and enjoyable, featuring exercises with fun names like the Hulk Slam and a Captain America move, which are excellent when involving your kids.

These HIIT workouts are designed for rapid fat loss, body sculpting, endurance, and cardio, while the lifting programs also support fat loss and muscle building and can boost your cardio. Ensure you're physically ready to take on these workouts; consult a doctor, if necessary, especially if you have injuries or medical conditions. Modifications can always be made to accommodate your specific needs.

For personalized guidance, my Lords are available to help tailor workouts to your specific goals. Planning is crucial—if not with us, pick a workout, learn the correct form via YouTube or an app, and get started. If you're engaged in jiu-jitsu, rock climbing, or other activities, schedule these on lighter days or in addition to your weightlifting routine.

I cannot emphasize the importance of consistent weightlifting—aim for at least five days a week, ideally seven. It might be tough. You might need to wake up an hour earlier. But whatever it takes, do it. We're here to achieve results fast. Rest days were designed for bodybuilders working four to six hours daily.

Remember **#MorrowMomentum**: Adding and subtracting is easy here.

An easy first step for your daily Instagram story post:
Take a photo of yourself at the gym and post it with:

DAY 1
Working Out
Meal Plan
No Alcohol
#MorrowMomentum
@cassfostermorrow

All Lord's Momentum and Lord's Transformation Resources:

Nutrition, Fitness, Guides, and Supplements are available at https://MorrowMarraige.com/Tools.

Skills:

After emphasizing health, let's pivot to skills—specifically, learning new ones. I've often said in The Reset that your wife has to meet when you are a 10. If you embody complete respect, it's tough for anyone to justify disrespect in return. One key aspect here is skill development. Many started as ambitious, driven men when we first met our wives. Over time, the pressures of climbing the career ladder or expanding a business, coupled with family responsibilities, might have dulled that edge. You might find yourself coasting, losing the drive that characterized your earlier self.

"Let's not forget the many of you that sit around and do nothing with your life, justifying your 'big' paycheck when you're not really earning."

I understand that life's demands can be overwhelming, but that's no reason to stop progressing. Developing new skills is crucial. For example, coaching your kid's football team is great, but why stop there? One of the Lords in our program doesn't just coach his own kids; he reaches out to coach teams in low-income areas where these boys lack role models. That's taking the initiative to a whole new level, aiming to shift social dynamics significantly. More on this later, but think about every skill you learn or 'thing' you're doing with your skills as a new add to your day count.

Remember, this doesn't have to be a massive undertaking. Let's say you learn to knit—not the most macho skill by traditional standards, but who cares? Imagine knitting a sweater, giving it to a homeless man, teaching him to sell it to a brand like Lululemon, and landing a job there. Suddenly, you've changed your life, sparked a chain of inspiration, and helped someone find their purpose. He will then want to help homeless people in return.

Imagine his Day Count on social media:

DAY 13
Working Out
No Alcohol
Learning to knit
Sales Training with Jeremy Minor

DAY 76–Post with homeless dude and inspirational post of giving him the sweater and helping him with his pitch.

DAY 186–Motivational post after signing the deal with Lululemon (who wanted the story for PR—BAD).

First, you need to get some skills. When thinking about your purpose and the mark you want to make in the world, you start by adding and subtracting things that allow you to gain momentum. I have a complete list of suggestions at https://MorrowMarraige.com/Tools but think of subtracting negative things like your coping mechanisms first. Then, add things like reading, listening to podcasts, or taking a specific course or mentoring in an area like the aforementioned sales training: Jeremy Minor's, 7th Level.

"Something that interests you and WILL MOVE YOU FORWARD."

Some practical skills to look at for your day count that can pad your wallet sooner will also be an avenue many men should take. Consider day trading or diving into the cryptocurrency market. With AI becoming a powerhouse tool, why not learn to code a bot that can trade for you, saving you the fees from third-party investors and potentially growing substantial wealth? What about Dave Ramsey's courses, from budgeting to financial freedom?

Some of you might be starting from scratch with no savings. That's exactly why you should be thinking about these opportunities. I've also seen 7 figure earners double their income because they applied the principles of The Reset in their business and used Momentum. This is no joke. What if you don't know where to start? That's the beauty of it; you don't need one. The direction may not be clear initially, but the goal is to start somewhere and be consistent.

Maybe your journey will lead you to join me in this mission. What skills do you possess? Maybe you're great at building websites but haven't tapped into developing apps or integrating AI. Perhaps there are men you can reach because you are/were an athlete. Do you have a background in oilfield or construction? I'm not necessarily reaching those men.

Some of you will know how to integrate your skills and blend them with The Reset, which could dramatically impact the bottom line of Fortune 500 companies. Have you thought of how your family has suffered through terrible hardship with a child's disability? You have a story and can learn skills to share your impact with the world.

"I cannot do this alone. The world needs leaders. Look around at the choices our governments are making these days."

The key here is that you choose something that genuinely interests you. I've provided plenty of resources that transformed my life; now it's your turn to use them to transform yours. Maybe you'll be inspired to help others with similar challenges, like a few of my clients who found a new purpose in partnering with me to create a youth program using Morrow Momentum.

One of my lords is creating a Christian version of this book and The Reset. Another is creating a bolt-on spiritual leadership program.

The possibilities are endless. We're talking about programs for men in prison, men and women exiting the military, and women (working with Kathryn). The time you take to learn skills is imperative in this journey, with or without partnering with me or Kathryn.

"Aim to change the world with your story and experiences. They need it."

This might seem intimidating and unnecessary. I assure you, it is necessary. What is crucial is that you start learning—now. Whether picking up a book, taking a course, or collaborating with peers on my app, your only objective is to keep rising; do NOT move backward again. Being a lifelong learner makes you more engaging and attractive—not just to your wife but to everyone around you. I cannot stress this enough. The testimonials from men and women in Morrow Momentum only amplified my work in The Reset and Kathryn's work in The White Picket Fence Project.

Get started. Don't wait until you figure out your entire life's purpose. Your path will become clearer as you learn and rise during Morrow Momentum. Start jotting down ideas, make plans, and take action. Every challenge you meet is an opportunity for growth. Be the man who learns, grows, and leads by example. Start now, right after you finish this book. Engage with fellow Lords, join the free coaching calls for Momentum at https://MorrowMarraige.com/Tools, share your ideas and utilize your combined skills to elevate each other. This is how you fully redefine yourself as a Man in Control, constantly evolving and never settling.

"NEVER go back to holding yourself back. Classic Nice Guy."

Legacy and Impact:

Embarking on a journey to expand your skills and enhance your value can be daunting. I get it. It's not just the challenge of mastering new domains; it's also about managing the expectations and adapting to the changes this growth brings, especially within your relationships.

For instance, dedicating time to personal development might be met with resistance from your wife, who might initially perceive your commitment as a diversion from family time. However, it's crucial to remember that leadership at home doesn't mean yielding to ease; it means steering towards growth for yourself and your family. Remember, your wife has a God-given purpose, too. You may need to lead her to it or at least guide her to identify it.

"I had to lead Kathryn to leading women."

Embracing this path requires not just ambition but a vision of legacy. This must always start with the concept of giving back—a principle that enriches others' lives and aligns you with a deeper sense of purpose. I'm not saying you can't make insane money from it. For most Nice Guys, filling your cup with giving without expectation will be key to stepping out of the Nice Guy Triangle.

For many, including myself, this has started in small, communal settings like church events or community service, like organizing holiday meals for the less fortunate. These acts of kindness are gateways to larger life changes I am pushing you towards. They shift your focus from self to 'full' service, creating a mindset that values contribution over convenience.

My coaching journey began similarly. It started with informal calls to help a man here and there. This sparked a deeper commitment to my passion and led me to harness social media to reach a broader audience. Each step built my confidence and clarity, transforming my initial interest into an obligation for impact, leading Kathryn and me to pursue other initiatives like the White Picket Fence Project and the Six-Figure Nap programs.

"Hitting men and women as a united front."

Momentum is about paying forward emotional strength. Remember, you and the world struggle with this. You're learning, sharing your willingness to step out of your comfort zone, and then sharing your pain with them. Your inspiration from your support is only secondary once you've accomplished and triumphed.

As men and women appreciate you for how you have suffered–just like them—-your relatability connects you. If you don't believe me, go back to the podcast episode, my free training, or social media content that connected you with me. You understand the clearest if you've been connected through our stories because of the gifting Kathryn and I do in any capacity.

Consider your mindset without Morrow Momentum. Every role, no matter how powerful it appears, does not actually hold the potential for significant impact. Whether you're a doctor saving lives or a mechanic ensuring safety through vehicle repairs, the doctor is no more valuable than the mechanic.

If the mechanic had not fixed the vehicle before the accident, the doctor would not have received his validation for saving a life. Reflect on what legacy you want to establish. How do you want to be remembered? For me, transforming men and women, I could never have reached alone, but more importantly, the people you and I can reach because of you.

"I mentioned Kathryn's 'awe' earlier: The love, respect, and adoration she aspires to deliver to the man I am at home, coupled with who I am in the world... Let's just say I know I am loved, needed, and desired."

Legacy is about living authentically, dreaming boldly, and continuously setting goals that challenge you to rise above baseline normal. Whether improving yourself, building relationships, or contributing to your community, these efforts propel you toward a more fulfilling existence. Start by reevaluating your priorities and embracing a life driven by purpose and impact. This isn't just about you or me—it's about setting a precedent for future generations, showing them that every effort counts and every person, including the people you will impact, has the potential to leave a lasting mark.

"It gives me chills."

Hobbies, Friends, and Family:

Discussing hobbies, friends, and family, we must discern which people in our lives extend from obligation, if they serve as unnecessary distractions, or if we should keep them with us. When people introduce negativity into your life, the impact can harm your success. This will be difficult to hear; hobbies, friends, and family are the last additions to your calendar. I'm not advocating for a life without hobbies, friends, or family—these should be sources of joy and positive energy. Whatever you fill your time with must positively contribute to your goals and values. Here are examples of how they can drain you instead and how you need to manage them as a Man in Control.

Consider common hobbies like obsessing over the NFL. I love it. It's a fantastic sport, but if your efforts in organizing game-day parties or spending on fan gear surpass your efforts for your wife, your wife will not feel like your priority. Or perhaps you play hockey six nights a week—it's super fun and a decent workout, but at what cost to family time? Another hobby might be restoring cars. My God, I love restomods and hot rods. While rewarding, if it consumes every weekend, it detracts from time with your family.

Conversely, there are beneficial hobbies. Take Jiu-Jitsu, for example; it's an excellent workout and teaches composure under pressure—traits you can apply across all life areas, enhancing your masculinity and importance, as discussed by Travis Neville in his book *The Ideal Man: Reviving Masculinity*. Such activities can significantly enhance intimacy with your wife, channeling your disciplined energy into passion. In the same spirit, you can often turn an otherwise playful hobby into something much bigger. Could you have underprivileged boys help you restore your car?

I want you to approach hobbies as opportunities to grow and improve yourself, not just as leisure activities. Focus on hobbies that build you up and make you a more intriguing and vibrant person. Many hobbies, like working out, can be scheduled long before your family even wakes up for the day.

Regarding friends and family, it's easy to feel obligated to maintain these relationships because they've been in your life forever. But if they're dragging you down, it's time to reassess. You might face guilt trips about family obligations or criticism from friends who notice you're changing. If these relationships create negativity, they hinder your progress. It's essential to maintain boundaries with those who detract from your growth. In Morrow Momentum, I describe this as removing the noise. Set boundaries, block them, and delete them from your life if needed.

Being ambitious and driven often means making hard choices about who and what you allow. "Remember my earlier reference to Brian Mark's comment on 'Proximity'. If a friend or family member doesn't support your journey towards becoming a better man—whether it's through discouraging your workouts or mocking your study time—it might be time to distance yourself from that negativity. The misaligned values of others should not compromise your goals and personal growth.

"Your wife is the exception. See earlier chapters."

This concept is about recalibrating your life to ensure that everything from your hobbies to your social circles propels you forward, not holds you back. This recalibration is crucial for becoming a Lord, a leader not just in your home but in every aspect of your life. It's about dropping unnecessary dead weight, whether it's a time-consuming hobby or a toxic relationship, and embracing practices that align with your core values, impact, and legacy. Remember, discipline isn't just a practice; it's a pathway to becoming the man you were born to be.

"Use caution. Do not get sucked into trying to lead someone you care about. Your job is not to convince someone. Your job is to lead them."

Directions for Lost Men: Finding Your Way Out of the Rabbit Hole:

Let's address this directly because I genuinely want to connect and empathize with many of you who feel lost. Over the years, you've likely felt defined by your roles as a husband, father, or career. While these are significant, there's so much more to you. If you've been involved in activities like volunteering at church, why not elevate your participation? Leadership is about initiative, not just participation. This distinction is crucial.

"If you and don't serve, then start with your selfishness there and at home. What? Do you just show up and take? If so, this means you are not special when you do serve."

Standing Out in Familiar Spaces:

Simply going through the motions doesn't cut it. For instance, while others might be content with routine contributions in church settings, why not approach the pastoral team with innovative ideas? Suggest new ways to engage the community, improve service delivery, or start a Lords (men's) group and partner with me to change lives. Leadership is about making impactful changes, not just filling roles.

"Now, you can bring The Reset to men and with the vulnerability I inspire to actually do something in your church."

That's a powerful day count for Momentum. Find out more at https://MorrowMarriage.com/Tools.

Leveraging Modern Tools to Rediscover Your Interests:

There are a million ways to get started. You should have learned by now that time can be managed. If money is an issue, start with YouTube; it's a treasure trove of inspiration. Search for hobbies or activities that resonate with your age group or interests. Learn for free. Curious about martial arts? Look beyond Jiu-Jitsu; there are numerous styles, each offering unique benefits and skills.

Use AI tools like ChatGPT to explore further. These platforms can offer suggestions faster and more tailored than traditional searches. For example, ask, "What are fun activities for someone in their 40s in [your city]?" AI can help brainstorm ideas, from opening a martial arts studio to serving underprivileged communities, even exploring side income opportunities.

Making Exploration Fun:

Remember, discovering your purpose should be exhilarating, not daunting. If it feels like fun, you'll naturally bring positive energy back home, enhancing the dynamic within your household. This shift can light the passion from the bottom of the Rejection Ladder, creating an attractive Green Light in your home.

Taking Action:

When you add things that will move you forward with Morrow Momentum and subtract things that are holding you back, you will begin to identify where you want to go with this. It happens naturally. You can also start by listing interests that catch your eye for things to add. Get excited about these possibilities! This list isn't just tasks; it's a map for your journey towards rediscovery. The impact will come.

Engaging with these new interests will refresh your confidence and make you a more attractive man to your wife. Get ready to STAT Respond and pay attention to your level of participation at home if you spend too much time putting effort into purpose and Momentum. Your journey is about sparking the qualities that initially made you exciting to your wife and others. This path you're carving is essential—it's about becoming a beacon of positivity and a man of inspiration.

"As a Lord, you will never be done rising."

Schedule It: How I Build Out My Life Calendar:

Let's get into how I meticulously schedule my life, keeping adaptability at the forefront, especially when compromising with my wife or challenges with the children. We've got our beautiful dating and sex life, kids' activities, work, impact/legacy, and our personal development, and now moving through the foster system to bring in at least three young men or women we can lead—all of which need careful planning in my calendar. Here's how I do it, ensuring I stay a Man at Home yet focused on growth.

Setting Time for Non-Negotiables:

First, I block out time for essentials like my workday and workouts. If you're still figuring out your routine, use that time to research effective workouts. You still put it in your calendar. This isn't wasted time; it's foundational for setting up a routine that sticks.

Everything from work hours to kids' activities is repeated in my calendar to ensure I'm organized and accountable.

Balancing Family Time and Personal Projects:

When it comes to our kids, not every activity needs to be on their schedule. I pick what allows for meaningful family time and personal attention for each of them. My wife and I share these responsibilities. One month, I might take the kids swimming while she handles dance classes, and we might switch the next. It keeps both of us actively involved and helps us manage our time better.

Integrating Personal Growth and Home Projects:

I also carve out time for ongoing personal projects, whether fixing up the house or diving into a new hobby that aids my growth. I schedule these consistently, often on weekends, to ensure they get the attention they deserve without overwhelming my weekdays. Pro Tip: get up earlier and work after they're all in bed. This is temporary.

Flexibility and Adaptation:

Life throws curveballs, and when it does, I adapt my schedule. If something new comes up, like a kid's activity or a request from Kathryn, I shuffle things around but keep my priorities intact. This adaptability is key to maintaining balance while pursuing my goals.

Consistency in Routine:

I'm up hours before my family every morning to hit the gym, go through goals, etcetera. Consistency here is crucial—it transforms my fitness routine from a chore to a vital part of my daily life. I set my alarm for 4:30 am every day and get moving, no excuses.

"Set an alarm for bedtime, not for waking up."

Leveraging Technology for Learning:

Learning is a daily priority. I use audiobooks during workouts or set aside specific times for reading. This constant intake of new information enriches my conversations and enhances my role as a leader at home and beyond.

Building a Legacy:

I also carve out time to give back to the community, aligning with my values and vision for a lasting legacy. Lately, this has been worldwide on social media platforms. Like my work or family commitments, these activities are scheduled and valued.

Executing the Plan:

Putting each of these activities on my calendar ensures that every aspect of my life is guided by purpose and intention. It's about more than managing time—it's about maximizing life and embodying the roles of Man with Purpose, Man at Home, and Man with Kids. This structured approach doesn't just prepare me for success; it integrates success into every day of my life. Additionally, playtime for Man at Play is scheduled; I also use blocks in my calendar for this.

"I live what I sell, and I sell A LOT because of it."

Bonus Hack:

I use an Apple Watch to keep me on track with alarms. It's the fastest way I know how. No matter who I am with, I can pause for a second and use an alarm to either get to it later or to make a note, reminder, or block in my calendar.

Take these steps, adapt them to your life specifics, and start crafting a schedule that meets and exceeds your potential. Let's build a life as ambitious and driven as we are.

"Whatever the reason you say you don't need a calendar or alarms, that is the exact reason you need them."

MANATPLAY

Go Get Your Wife.

Man at Play

"You hug your friends and kiss your kids; your marriage is the only place for mad passion."

The moment you've all been waiting for Man at Play, my favorite man. This is what it's all about. We're racing for that checkered flag, reigniting the passion and fire that the whole Reset aims to restore. You've laid the foundation throughout every preceding chapter, sharpening your skills.

But before I dive deeper, here is a crucial reminder: if you haven't fully committed to the earlier chapters, you need to double back and ensure all those foundational steps are solidly in place. If you're not fully embodying the roles of Man in Power, Man in Control, Man with Impact, Man at Home, Man with Kids, and Man with Purpose, then you won't succeed as a Man at Play.

Many of you have eagerly anticipated this section, perhaps even skipping ahead. However, it's vital to understand that Man at Play is not standalone; it's the culmination of everything that's come before. If you've skimped on earlier responsibilities or half-heartedly applied the lessons, now is the time to revisit them. This man completes the Passion Pillar and is designed to make your wife try to run you off track, challenge you, and test your intentions until she chases you to the bedroom.

"When men join Lords in The Reset, it's not uncommon for them to go through the whole course four times at a bare minimum. I

could not deliver everything from The Reset in this book, so ensure you read it multiple times before you commit fully to this chapter."

Now, let's set the stage. Depending on how fast you got through this book, your wife might undoubtedly feel smothered as you become more proactive and present in your relationship. It's a natural response to the positive changes you're implementing. You'll likely encounter her resistance if you show up as I've instructed, apply the lessons, and genuinely engage with the process. It's not necessarily a setback but a sign that you're pushing the right buttons and initiating real change.

Here's what you need to consider: each lesson, each role you've learned, stacks upon the others. They intertwine and build upon one another so that you are equipped, ready, and resilient when you reach this chapter—Man at Play. You know why you're asking her out on a date, why you're planning those special moments, and why you're steering the relationship towards passion and intimacy.

Remember, if your efforts in romance seem to fail, it's likely because of unresolved issues or resentment. These emotional barriers cannot be skipped; they must be addressed with sincerity and patience. If your wife is holding onto past hurts or if there's lingering bitterness, the strategies of Man at Play won't just fail you; you will fall flat.

You need to be your best, most authentic self—a man who's grown through his experiences and emerged stronger, more engaged, and more committed than ever. When you purchase my course, I delay each man in each pillar over a precise drip process in The Reset. Here, you could have read this book straight through in a day.

The Reset is designed to help you practice and hone your skills. With the drip, we can use your reflections and real-life stories within coaching to move you forward. If you're rushing this process, please be aware.

If you've been attentive and true to the Reset's process, let's dive into the Passion Pillar's components—A Man with Purpose transitions to the Lover, the Player, and the Magnet. Your role as a Lover is to make your wife feel loved, valued, and respected. You use your created environment to make your wife feel truly seen and heard.

The Player brings excitement and fun, injecting humor and lightheartedness into your interactions, which is crucial for breaking down the last of the walls and building intimacy. Lastly, the Magnet is about creating that irresistible pull-through emotional tension—drawing her in with your newfound confidence and vitality. He may need to be firm and assertive while maintaining the Lover's gentleness, still providing the Player with adventure and fun.

Embrace the role of Man at Play with all the seriousness and dedication it deserves. It's about strategically cultivating a deep, passionate connection with your wife that recreates the mad passion in marriage you once had. Let's light those fires and show her the man she fell in love with, who can navigate any challenge and turn any setback into an opportunity for growth and deeper connection.

Rejection Ladder Part II:

When handling rejection, knowing the Lover, the Player, and the Magnet's different styles is crucial. Additionally, remembering the Rejection Ladder, it's imperative to always know your position. When you're not climbing higher on the ladder, this typically means the lower rungs aren't quite secure.

You must maintain your power, control, and impact consistently. Feeling the sting when your wife runs into the side of your car can unleash a torrent of insecurity. But remember, none of that will matter when your wife adores you and cannot resist you. It's about keeping your pace on the track, lap after lap, until you get that checkered flag repeatedly.

You're in charge of maintaining a Green Light, even when rejection stings and it's attractive when you do. Showing frustration, annoyance, or neediness—like a child having a tantrum—will never appeal to your wife. You need to always embody confidence and control. If you become needy or pouty after a rejection, you're not the strong, confident man she needs. If she says she needs space, or you're smothering her, understand that if you're following the program, this might just be a test, unconscious or not.

"There is a possibility that she believes you are trying to manipulate or control her. This is highly probable if you've heard that with prior actions from earlier actions."

Now, let's dissect the rejection ladder further. You don't necessarily need to hit every rung before sex happens, but understanding the rungs you're missing can guide your approach. If your wife seems cold or distant, it doesn't necessarily mean a retreat; it signals a need to assess and adapt. You should always be aware of your position on this ladder; it's not just about managing rejection—it's about strategic positioning and your momentum. Remember what STAT Responses are for, providing structure for the direction you want to go.

Consider some common scenarios: Your wife might ignore your attempts at conversation, perhaps absorbed in her phone or visibly upset. First, read the room. She might be busy or stressed, not disinterested or cold. No expectations, remember? If she's unresponsive, continue your actions or engage the kids in a fun activity. If she's stressed or snapping, show understanding and do what you will do without frustration. It shows you're attentive and caring, traits of a true Lover.

What if your gestures, like texts or gifts, are met with silence or a "Whatever" response? Do not hold your covert contracts—expecting something in return for your actions. You give because you love her, not to receive immediate gratitude or validation. It doesn't diminish your gift if she seems indifferent to a gift or a loving note. For now, it's about giving without immediate expectations.

Handling more direct rejections, especially in physical advances, requires finesse. Don't get upset if she rejects a flirt or an intimate touch. Instead, use it as a playful moment. For instance, if a compliment isn't reciprocated, or a playful squeeze is met with a rejection, keep it light. Say something humorous like, "Guess I should have brushed my teeth," or if a hug is declined, playfully suggest, "Oh, thank God. I'm too hot right now, anyway. Should we turn the heat down?" Smile and move on.

During a Lords coaching session a year or so ago, I shared how Kathryn and I had a planned sex weekend, but she rejected me later that evening. We had a crazy day at the hotel, and Kathryn wasn't good to go for round four. It was a rare moment for us, as Kathryn rarely expressed disinterest, and it brought up old insecurities for me.

Instead of reacting negatively, I kept the mood light and fun, which, after a few hours, led to her initiating. It highlighted an essential truth: handling rejection with humor and levity can transform a potentially painful moment into an opportunity for a deeper connection.

"She jumped me in the middle of the night."

Rejection isn't just about what happens in those moments; it's about how you respond and continue to engage. Each interaction is a step on the ladder. Don't sulk or withdraw if a physical gesture like cuddling is rejected. Instead, make a light joke or offer to do something together: "I'm starving. Do you need a sandwich?" This approach maintains the connection and keeps the atmosphere positive.

Handling rejection effectively means always being ready to respond positively to flip a potential conflict into an opportunity. Transforming her rejections into an opportunity for growth, connection, and, eventually, a deeper, more connected relationship.

"Ultimately, connected desire."

The Player and The Magnet can step up your game and help you 'Act like you just got laid' as you embody the core value. Staying consistent and not taking her rejections so personally will move you around the track fast. Coupled with being a highly valuable Man with Purpose… you see why we're winning races over in Lords.

Romance:

Romance—what is it, and how do you use it effectively? Let's simplify it. At its core, romance is the mystery and excitement that surrounds love. Too many people complicate what romance should look like; it's straightforward. It's about being thoughtful and affectionate in ways that resonate with both of you. You don't need to mimic the over-the-top gestures found in smut romance novels or romantic comedies, though they have their charm.

"Focus on the simple acts that signify your love and attention by keeping her guessing and making her feel good."

Many men tell me, "I'm just not good at romance," but I urge you to kick your limiting belief. Romance is within every man's grasp—the way you show affection, the thoughtful little gestures that make her feel special. That's where the real magic of romance lies. It's not about grand gestures but about the everyday actions that show you care and pay attention, as long as you aren't robotic.

Consider it this way: romance is for getting your wife's attention. If she's not already looking your way, simply giving flowers or gifts won't always work. These should not be seen as apologies or obligations but as genuine expressions of your feelings. Your approach must be sweet and thoughtful if you're working your way up the ladder. Compliment her meaningfully, flirt playfully, and understand if she's hesitant—it might just be where her mind is now.

Suppose your wife has historically been indifferent or even resistant to romance. In that case, it's likely not because she dislikes romance but because it has never been presented in a way that resonated with her. Maybe past gestures felt forced or were gross with expectations. This should stand out to you by now. Think about integrating romance into your everyday interactions—make it a natural extension of your affection for her.

For instance, let's talk about timing, which can be crucial. I remember buying Kathryn a mixer she had wanted for ages. It was perfect—red, expensive, exactly what she talked about. But when I gave it to her during a hectic time, she just said, "Thanks." The timing was off; she had too much on her mind with her master's program and other stressors. Timing isn't always about waiting for or setting up the perfect moment but about being sensitive to her current state and environment.

Romance can also mean understanding when not to push. If she's been dealing with the kids all day and feels touched out, recognize that. She might still need space even if you've been attentive all day. That has nothing to do with you. This is where reading the room becomes essential—it's synonymous with being a good Lover; you're attuned to her responses and needs.

Lastly, avoid making common mistakes mentioned in Ah Ha moments. For example, touching her inappropriately without context or sending 'dick' pics abruptly can be turn-offs. These actions miss the mark on romance—it's about building anticipation, not just physical gratification.

"After over 1000 women in Kathryn's program, most don't want to see your dick. She'll tell women to send pics to you—but you're not your sexy, hot wife."

Think of romance as a bridge that connects your daily interactions to deeper intimacy and understanding. It's about making her feel loved, valued, and seen—not just as a wife or a mother—and not your sex doll—but as the woman you fell in love with. Keep refining your approach and keep her feelings and needs in mind. You'll find that romance can be a powerful tool in strengthening your relationship. I encourage you to bounce ideas off of other (loving) men since this is foreign to most.

"You get good at what you practice."

Hacks:

I want to share a couple of mindset hacks that are game changers. These aren't just tricks; they're foundational shifts that can deeply influence how you and your wife interact, enhancing the dynamics as you embrace the role of Man at Play.

Best Friend Hack: This one's close to my heart. You and I are working towards being your wife's best friend again, right? But what if she's not there yet? Think back to when you both clicked instantly effortless and exciting. That's our target. Next time she has a bad day, instead of getting frustrated, approach her with the empathy and support you would for your best friend. Even on a date that feels awkward, keep in mind that she's your best friend. This mindset helps you stay supportive and empathetic, no matter her mood.

"If you wouldn't do this with your best friend, revisit Ah Ha Moments: Wit as a Weapon, and rethink the entire Man with Purpose section."

I Love You Hack: How you say "I love you" matters immensely. Say it like you mean it with the full force of your conviction. You're a Lord, remember? When you tell your wife you love her, let it carry the power and certainty that defines your love. It's not just about the words;

it's about how you make her feel when you say them—valued, loved, irreplaceable.

Name Her Hack: Names matter more than we often realize. Pay close attention to how your wife reacts to different pet names. If she lights up when you call her "Sweetheart" but cringes at "Babe," then you know what to do. Tailor how you address her to reflect her preferences, showing her that you're attentive and that you care deeply about her feelings. This isn't just about making her smile; it's about making her feel seen and heard in the smallest details of your interactions.

"If she's in the stage of, 'Don't call me X, I'm done,' do not listen to her. Default to what you used to call her. If you're lost, use what she would call you."

These hacks are more than just strategies; they express your commitment and love. Implement them with care, and watch as they enrich the connection between you and your wife, aligning perfectly as you level up as a Man at Play.

The Lover and The Player:

Lords often get confused between the Lover, the Player, and the Magnet due to the overwhelming disconnect between them and their wives. Yet, the core ideas are quite straightforward—If you want your wife to feel as adored as you've said you are for her, thrilled and ready to feel how she felt when you were both younger and free, you're on the right track. I've actually tricked you. You have been secretly learning to be all three throughout this book.

"Now we're going to go deeper."

Let's set the scene. We're past the phase of routine gestures like bringing home flowers or cards. Those are expected and ordinary. I heard countless men at my gym express confusion over what romance truly means, reflecting a widespread misunderstanding, supported by hundreds of women saying their husbands didn't get it. So here's a richer, more vibrant approach to reigniting that spark, blending the roles of a Lover and a Player.

Being a Lover and a Player with Flowers and Cards:

A Lover brings home roses with a card saying, "Hey babe, I love you so much. I'm thankful you're my wife, and inserts the reason why." That's standard, but we're not about standard here. Let's level that up. Imagine a Lover picking these roses because they signify a particular appreciation or recognition of something she has done or said. Not out of obligation but celebration. That is the (inserted) why.

Now, the Player doesn't just bring any flowers; he brings her favorite ones, arranged by him in a vase, accompanied by a beautifully crafted card that goes beyond "I love you." It's about personalization and genuine thoughtfulness, reflecting a deep understanding of her tastes and preferences. He'll use the Lover's List but deliver it in a sexy way.

Using Music to Connect:

Music is universally powerful. As a Lover, notice what she listens to, perhaps a repeated track. Use that. Invite her to dance to that song, creating an intimate, shared moment. As a Player, create a modern-day mixtape, a playlist of songs she adores, and surprise her. Maybe you even dance with her, making the moment about the music and your physical connection.

Elevating the Simple Massage:

Anyone can give a casual leg rub while lounging on the couch, a nice Lover's gesture, especially after a hard day. I do this (often) daily for Kathryn. It rewards her hard work at the gym and shows that I appreciate her body. But a Player? He throws in an accent and gets goofy when he does it and has no expectation of sex—and has no need to tell her that. He can tell if she's ready to go or too far into relaxation.

Gift-Giving that Resonates:

Then there's the approach to gifts. It's easy to buy jewelry—the expected gift. But understanding her desires, like finding that unique yellow antique stone she's mentioned in passing, is being a true Lover. A Player, however, would go a step further, customizing a setting around that stone, creating a piece of jewelry that's not just beautiful but deeply meaningful.

Communication as a Lover and a Player:

Texting can seem mundane, but as a Lover, you send texts that show you're thinking of her. A Player, however, uses these moments to create a story or share a memory—perhaps pulling over to take a photo with something that reminded him of her, making it visual and visceral. Both a Lover and a Player can step it up by sending an audio message to express tone and/or a video message to express tone and body language.

The Art of Complimenting:

Compliments are simple yet powerful. A Lover notices her across the room and compliments her appearance or the effort she's put into her look that day. A Player makes it more intense by complimenting her and doing so in an unexpectedly bold or intimate way, like whispering in her ear rather than shouting across the room.

Each of these scenarios blends the everyday with the extraordinary, transforming mundane moments into peaks of emotional intimacy. It's about understanding the subtle art of being both a Lover and a Player, making each interaction not just an act of love but a playfully engaging moment that leaves her both comforted and intrigued.

"This is how you reignite the spark, by being inventive, attentive, and above all, genuine in every gesture you make."

The Magnet:

These traits are essential to master and make your own. There isn't a one-size-fits-all formula here; it's about flipping positive emotional tension from the negative. You might wonder why there's a specific section for the Magnet but not for the Lover and the Player.

Firstly, you need to be a Lover. Secondly, bring the fun; using STAT and handling rejection like a Lord makes you the Player. Remember, girls just want to have fun. They still sing Cyndi Lauper's song today. This should be the theme throughout The Reset, and the Magnet is where you start applying it. Read this several times and begin shifting your mindset to understand how women think versus how men think. It's about masculine versus feminine dynamics, and the mindset shifts I present will naturally handle a lot of the work for you.

The Magnet is all about polarity—drawing her in like a Magnet. Keep this in mind before diving into the rest of this section, and you will embody this role rapidly. Once you embody the Magnet, the Player can bring fun, curiosity, and mystery. Is this starting to click for you as you think back to the Adventure in STAT Responses now?

Romance involves mystery and excitement, wrapped in love. The mystery aspect involves variety and novelty. Avoid always doing the same things. Excitement comes from anticipation and uncertainty. Many wives, like Kathryn, may not like surprises and get anxious, which is also polarity. I don't surprise Kathryn often because it makes her very anxious, but it creates positive tension when appropriate. With variety, we ensure frequency and consistency because we are like diamonds, constantly providing this overarching polarity, giving her what she needs.

You're not going to tell her everything. You might say, "The black romper, Friday Night, 9 pm," and leave the rest a mystery. This approach won't work with every wife, so you need to gauge her reactions and remember your STAT Responses. Handle rejection like a Lord and keep moving forward. Let's dive into variety, frequency, and consistency.

I developed the VFC method—Variety, Frequency, and Consistency. You're always coming up with new ideas. I provide many ideas, but you should find what works for you. This needs to be authentic for both you and your wife. It doesn't mean everything you do will be perfect for her, but you should care about what she loves. Don't just go to the same five restaurants or have movie nights repeatedly. That's boring. Engage constantly to keep variety going. Use a variety of ways to say, "I love you," or share a compliment. Sometimes, it's a love note, a text message, a video message, or a surprise visit to the office. We'll find out what works for you and where you need to be in your marriage.

Consistency is crucial. Frequency is equally important. You need to do this continually and with variety, so it doesn't feel overwhelming for her. Maybe, two times a week, you do something special. I'd love to do something for Kathryn every day, but it's not realistic nor necessary for my wife. Proper use of my Lovers List works for my 'Words of Affirmation Wife'---Know your wife, but more on that soon. You need to read the room and ask for help from Lords on the app based on how much your wife asks for space and how out of control you are. Remember, some of this could be just a test. You'll have to STAT Respond, handle rejection, and keep structure forward and future paced. Consistency is key because men often give up when faced with rejection. Women need attention. It might not seem like it right now, but they do. Using your Lover's List to give affirmations shows you see her deeply.

Women want to be seen and heard. The Lover makes her feel loved, valued, and respected. She feels heard when you listen to her and act on what she says. When you give affirmations from your Lover's List, explaining why she's intelligent, fun, or beautiful, she knows you're looking deeper.

"Just don't let her lead you away from the direction you are moving."

For example, "When you wore that red dress, it looked stunning. My God, you lit up the world and I could see the work you've been putting in at CrossFit. The way it hangs on your hips perfectly." This attention and affirmation are vital, but avoid being overbearing or needy. Using the VFC method authentically will make a huge difference.

Understand that women need attention from confident, non-needy men. You are a Man at Play. Competition and status work here, too. As a Man with Purpose, you are valuable and give her attention, provide mystery, and show up as a playful man. This makes you stand out. When you're the 1%, leveling up while men everywhere are not, even if your wife is having an affair, the other guy will start slipping up if he hasn't already.

They all do. He will do the same things wrong I've shown you in this book, and she will eventually compare. Your wife will realize what she's turning down. Competition is real and draws women in.

"Even if your wife is not having an affair, don't take this lightly."

Compliments and attention make her feel good about herself. Buy her that dress she admired. Recently, Kathryn loved a dress someone wore. We found out about the brand and bought it online, and it felt like a fun date. It was for our sex weekend, and we went out for a drink and ordered the dress. Why? Because she's competitive. When she wears it, it looks even better on her. I also won the competition. Not only would many men never stop to do that in the moment, but they would not follow through and find the dress.

Drama, intrigue, and escape are crucial. I watch reality shows with Kathryn because she enjoys them. They provide drama, which she needs to get out of her system; Most women do. Listen and be her rock when she shares stories about her co-worker or friend.

You are a Man with Impact. This release flips negative tension. As a bonus, you will eventually find humor in reality shows. When you know what I teach you, watching reality TV, you want to DM every man from the shows just to help them. Maybe you should help me get in touch with them!

"Revisit Man with Purpose. I can't do this alone."

Intrigue and escape involve planning exciting, fun dates. Think about what would be exhilarating for you both and make them happen. Dominance and submission also play a role. Many men fear being themselves, especially around strong women. But even the most controlling women don't want to lead at home. Embrace your masculine role and understand the dynamic of dominance and submission. It doesn't have to be complicated. Simple acts like telling her what to do, like saying "Don't touch that door." And then opening it for her. Asking her to get you a drink when she's already going to the fridge or "Give me your leg (for a rub)" reinforces this dynamic.

"I like to stop Kathryn periodically and gently, but firmly, 'take' my affection."

As a Man at Play, the roles of a Lover, Player and Magnet will overlap. Think about creating positive emotional tension naturally, without rigid steps. Your wife might test you and try to provoke you, but you focus on what works. Understand the masculine versus feminine dynamics as you progress as a Man at Play.

The Real 5 Part I: My Take on the 5 Love Languages:

Here is an introduction to the Real Five, my adaptation to The Five Love Languages. If you're unfamiliar with them, Gary Chapman has written extensively on using the five love languages to connect more deeply with your partner. The premise is simple: each person has one or two primary love languages. When their partner expresses love in these languages, it resonates more deeply with them because it's communicated in a way they understand. Knowing your wife's language makes you reach her much faster.

However, it's crucial to understand something new here. Many men make the mistake of hitting the mark with their wife's love language, thus expecting their own love languages to be reciprocated. Now, as a Man in Control, you need to remember that the Five Love Languages are designed for giving love, not receiving it, at least from your perspective. Otherwise, you are headed for keeping score. Using Man with Impact, we can hold our wife accountable, but I will not head down any accountability path without knowing that a man is a Lord and out of the Nice Guy Triangle.

If you and your partner read the book or take the quiz together, you might expect that if you give her love in her language, she should give you love in yours. This can lead to frustration. Instead, be a Man in Power. Focus on controlling your actions and how you use her language, not how she uses yours. So, let's approach the Five Love Languages differently with my version, The Real 5.

I'll show you my way of using them later, but for now, let's review the Five Love Languages.

Words of Affirmation:

This tops my list because I believe most women value words of affirmation. Even if your wife isn't primarily a words of affirmation person, it's essential to use them. If she's been undermined, belittled, or criticized, especially during disagreements or arguments, words of affirmation can help rebuild her confidence and self-worth.

"Remember Kathryn's warning: "In marriage, 700 positives to one negative." Just get started."

Using the Lover's List, you can give real, meaningful affirmation. Instead of a generic compliment like, "Kathryn, you look gorgeous," be specific: "I love how you did your hair today; it's the perfect angle for this perfect shot on our date. Up there for thinkin', down there for dancing. Always on." She'll remember these words because they show genuine appreciation and recognition. This is the attention she needs and the Lover/Player effect we aim for.

Quality Time:

This one is straightforward: spend time together. However, it's not quality time if you're always on your phone or distracted. You need undistracted, meaningful interaction. Quality time isn't about passively watching TV together; it's about connecting. For example, when Kathryn and I watch TV, we make it quality time by pausing to talk about the show and maintaining physical touch. Make sure whatever you do together is engaging and creates connection. It's not uncommon for Kathryn and I to spend three hours watching a 45-minute show.

Acts of Service:

Acts of service can be tricky because they often blend into daily responsibilities. However, going above and beyond is what counts. For instance, if your wife is busy and you know she hasn't placed the Instacart order, take care of it for her. Doing tasks she dislikes or helping out more than usual shows you care and are invested in her well-being. Drive her to meet friends, open doors, and handle chores she hates. This not only helps her but also shows your involvement and support. A secret weapon when you master Man with Purpose, Morrow Momentum, and the Magnet is in how and when you balance dropping what you have going on to be there to serve her by saying no when you can't. This amplifies quality time.

Giving Gifts:

Gift-giving goes beyond just buying things. It's about thoughtful, meaningful gestures. Listen to what your wife admires or desires, and surprise her with it. For example, Kathryn wanted a specific locket that was hard to find, so I had it custom-made for her. This shows I listen to and value her. Thoughtful gifts can still make her feel loved and appreciated even if she's not primarily a gift-receiving person.

Physical Touch:

Most women are not primarily physical touch, but it's still important. For men, physical touch often equates to feeling desired. If your wife is a physical touch person, make it a point to touch her often. Compliment her while touching her face or shoulder, squeeze her bum, or hold her hand. If she isn't a physical touch person, incorporate it into your interactions to maintain intimacy.

These are the Five Love Languages, each crucial in their own way. Next, you'll learn how to stack them, combining the roles of Lover, Player, and Magnet to create a more profound connection. This approach will give you a wealth of inspiration and practical steps to enhance your relationship. Consider this your homework: start focusing on these aspects and thinking creatively about applying them in the Real Five.

"Let's dive into stacking the love languages by being a Lover, a Player, and a Magnet. This has been my adaptation of Gary Chapmen's work."

The Real 5 Part II: Stacking Love Languages:

Sometimes, you won't embody all three roles, but you'll always use at least two. You must understand your wife's love language(s); this is crucial. You need to reach your wife with the love you're presenting. However, by stacking the love languages, we can make this process more fun and inspirational. We want to inspire and lead while inviting your wife into these moments and events. This makes dates more exciting and easier to plan, too.

"As you practice, stacking love languages will become second nature."

Real 5 Examples:

Words of Affirmation and Giving Gifts:

Let's start with Kathryn as an example. She loves Pilates and looks great in her leggings. Combining words of affirmation and giving gifts could look like this: I know she likes to shop at Lululemon and wants specific leggings. So, I buy the leggings and say, "Baby, wow, your body's looking tight. I appreciate your hard work at Pilates and am so proud of you. You're always putting your all into it, so I got you this." Let her open the box—Boom! You've combined two love languages effectively.

Quality Time and Acts of Service:

Consider this scenario: I pick up ingredients for Kathryn's favorite meal on my way home. We spent quality time together making the meal, and then I told her to relax with a bath while I cleaned up the kitchen. This seamlessly combines quality time and acts of service. Truthfully, I would prefer my service to be rubbing her down while she is in the bath, and the dishes will be taken care of tomorrow.

Words of Affirmation and Physical Touch:

Let's use it here. Imagine scrubbing your wife in the tub. You say, "Hey babe, I can't believe how well you handled the kids' tantrums today. You are the mama of mamas. I'm blessed to have you as a partner. Thank you, baby." Then, direct her to the bath and offer to scrub her down, providing relaxation after a tough day.

Physical Touch and Quality Time:

If you walk past your wife and think she looks gorgeous, say, "Wow, baby, you look beautiful. Come here." Kiss her and start dancing with her. You could put some music on your phone and make it a real dance, but sometimes it's spontaneous. For instance, if we're driving and I'm holding Kathryn's hand, we're already with who we want to be with (Kathryn's line). I pull over, and we dance to a song on the radio or one I put on. I've also noticed (in my work) that this combination—of physical touch and quality time—can help break a wife free from insecurity, making your wife feel unapologetically herself.

Gift Giving and Acts of Service:

Suppose your wife and her best friend are excited about a concert. You give her tickets and say, "I want you to take Cindy, and I'll drive you guys so you don't have to worry about anything." This combines gift-giving and acts of service. You show you're comfortable and supportive by encouraging her to enjoy herself and providing the freedom to do so.

Go back and reread this section. Then, write out these examples, identifying the roles of the Lover, Player, and Magnet. Break down what each role entails in the scenarios. Be creative and notice the overlaps, but understand the distinct roles. If you cannot identify them, you will not master Man at Play.

Remember:

Lover: Makes his wife feel loved, valued, respected, seen, and heard.

Player: Makes her feel like a woman, ensuring she knows it's fun. She is his woman; he is her man.

Magnet: This character often overlaps with the Player when dealing with rejection and will gently yet assertively tell her what to do.

Play out the scenarios in your mind and understand how each role fits. Share your ideas with Lords in the app, even if they differ slightly from my examples. Have fun with this process. Your life and relationship will become much easier when you grasp the roles naturally. Take your time and enjoy the fun, winning along the way.

7 TYPES OF DATES

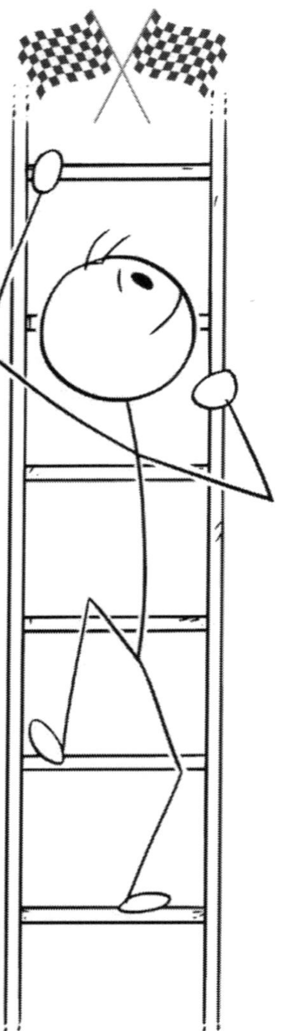

DEDICATED PLAY TIME AT LEAST ONCE PER WEEK - LONGER.
SHORTER PLAY TIME AT LEAST 2-3 TIMES PER WEEK.

SEX DATES

OVERNIGHT AND 2 DAYS, AT LEAST ONCE PER QUARTER. TRIPS, ONCE PER YER. BRING HELP IF YOU NEED TO BRING THE KIDS.

OVERNIGHTS/2 DAYS/TRIPS

SURPRISE HER WITH EXTRA STOPS.

TRAINCATIONS

DON'T GO TO THE SAME SPOTS. MINIMUM ONCE PER WEEK. GET HER OUT OF MOM-MODE.

DATE NIGHT OUT

MAKE MINI-DATES LONGER AT 1-2 TIMES PER WEEK. PREFERABLY EVERY DAY. MIX IT UP.

HOME DATES

3-10 MINUTES A DAY. MIX IT UP.

MINI-DATES

The Seven Types of Dates:

If you've made it this far, this won't sound surprising. Some common limiting beliefs about dating are that we don't have money for dates or that we have no one to take the kids.

During COVID-19, when we weren't even allowed to leave our houses, broke, and with no support, I came up with the Seven Types of Dates.

"Stop listening to everyone around you."

There are seven types of dates: mini-dates, home dates, date nights, traincations, nights away, weekends or week trips, and sex dates. If we want decades of happiness, we need to be having fun. If we're going to be best friends and lovers, we need to be exciting. Girls just want to have fun. Girls want adventure, and we want to give that positive emotional tension. The good "Drama." You just want to have a great freakin' time. This will be awkward for so many of you in the beginning.

It will also be a significant rejection phase for many of you, especially with all the different types of dates that I'm going to share. Now, far too many men, myself included, let our wives plan everything. Remember, she ran the home, the schedule, the dates, who we were going out with, what we were doing, whether we were going on dates, and when we were having sex.

Now, you need to really think: What does my wife like? What do I like? How can we both be unapologetically ourselves? Even if we talk about mini dates, if we're having a quick conversation, that won't necessarily be fun right now, but you're structuring future-paced.

If Kathryn comes to talk to me for one of our mini-dates, it might be something like, "Hey babe, do you want to hear something funny?" which sparks 10 minutes of great conversation.

You'll notice I won't give you a million different date ideas. I will give you a formula, and I want you to apply it because there's no sense in me giving thousands of men what Kathryn and I love to do. There is no sense in offering a few things that I've heard other men like to do with their wives. I want you to start being a great Lover. You will start to figure out what is great for the two of you and start being a Player to get her to want to go on these dates. Then be a Magnet and pull her in.

We will also have to deal with a lot of rejections. Now, you're going to be planning dates, thinking ahead, trying things out, and getting rejected. This is frustrating when you start really planning a great night out or a weekend away. You have babysitters ready; you even figured out and told her what she should wear. It's frustrating when you get rejected, and yes, you still need to do all that stuff.

Side note: you may not always have to do this. Kathryn handles most of our dates. She absolutely loves doing it. Remember, when we talk about each of our strengths, Kathryn is much better at planning that stuff than I am, and your wife probably is too. But in the beginning, we need to get things started. This is not unlike when you may have to do more around the house as a Man at Home right now. Most of you just need to get the ball rolling again.

What do we do when our wife rejects us? The basic premise is that we will do whatever we invite her to do without her. That's very, very important. The reason is simple: she has to meet you when you are a 10. If you're super fun and exciting and she wants to be cranky, sit on the couch and tell you to get lost. That can't last forever. We will continue to be a Man in Control, a Lord, and follow through.

As diamonds, we will go on a date and try to handle it in different ways, but all very similar. The premise is we're going to respond immediately. Your wife might tell you you're selfish or you look silly or stupid, but you know where you're going. You're providing the direction and structure of the marriage.

"Caution: I don't know your story. Some men I coach, I would NOT advise them to go out when she rejects him. Especially when suggesting overnight dates."

It's pretty straightforward. Dates require two components: Fun and spark. In other words, be exciting. Your wife needs to have an opportunity to interact and be interested. Right now, it's a bonus if you can make her feel like a woman. Get her out several times a month, dressed up and with no kids. This is how you get her out of Mom-Mode, and into Woman-Mode. Get her more in her feminine if your wife rejects you, STAT Respond.

Most importantly, do not limit yourself with three fast rejections: "She doesn't want to." We have no childcare." We don't have money for dates."

Mini-Dates:

We came up with mini-dates during COVID-19 due to the lockdowns. This was very awkward because we were stressed out after losing everything, even our home. We got evicted from the place we lived in a year after downgrading. This is where we came up with the idea, which was simple. Three to five minutes every single day, sometimes 10 minutes, when we can come together and connect.

So much of married time is just running past each other in the house, but if you can stop and turn it into at least a three to five-minute or a 10-minute connection phase, you can remind your wife that she is your priority. You may start with three times a week, depending on your rejections.

Home Dates:

I like having home dates, at least, one to three times a week. Kathryn and I do this seven days a week. This is anywhere from 20 minutes to an hour, and hey, if it's going well, you can spend hours together having a great time. These are extensions of mini-dates or planned dates at home. If you're extending a mini-date, take whatever you're doing on the mini-date and build on it. For example, let's say you're having a little dance for a mini-date, and then all of a sudden, that turns into listening to music for hours and just having some great laughs. We were stuck during COVID-19, just like you. Like us, many of you could have thrived at that time.

Date Night Out:

At least once a week, you need to have an actual date night. You must get your wife out of the house. You have to go to different places and do different things. You're trying different restaurants; you're trying different themes. Be exciting. Look at the events calendar for your city or use Chat GPT to find out new ideas. I have training on this: https://MorrowMarriage.com/Tools.

Traincations:

Traincations are fun because you surprise your wife with extra stops after you're already out. This is Player and Magnet to the max. Your wife, out of Mom Mode, wants to have fun. When you handle it, surprise her in her glory. When you do this right, she will be excited. It's important to note that even my dates with Kathryn are almost always filled with Traincations. I have zero expectations, and that's a good thing. She's usually in "Meet awesome people mode," and who knows what will happen.

"Sex is rarely on the table after date night or Traincations." Check your Man in Control."

Another reason Traincations are phenomenal is that they're a great way to flip the tone if your wife is triggered on a date and you need to STAT. Let's say you made it through dinner. You used STAT, but your wife's still not in the zone. Let's say, "Hey babe, come with me." With an outstretched hand, grab hers and take her to the next stop.

I'll walk downtown and see what's going on. With other people around, the energy is already different. If your wife is not really feeling it, she definitely wants to be distracted from you. Other people can help with that, even strangers; it's remarkable.

Go have fun with her. The Player doesn't mind talking to strangers, and as a Lover, you'll still "Check-in" with your wife. As a Player, you'll have fun when you do. Your wife will see you as the valuable Lord you are, and whether she SAFE reacts or tests you, STAT until she joins you on your adventure.

Overnights, Weekends, and Trips:

Plan them, do them as needed, and make them happen. Remember, one day your children will move away. Make time for you and your wife when you are alone for extended periods. You may struggle if your wife is like Kathryn; she hates being away from the kids. We plan weekends where we bring teenage babysitters and still see our children throughout the weekend. We still have plenty of time together and are very intentional about our alone time. I recommend it at least every quarter. As long as you care for your wife's emotional needs and not have her worried about the kids, you will connect on a deeper level.

Sex Dates:

There are many ways to talk about this based on where you are resetting mad passion in your marriage. Kathryn and I know we are having sex every night after the kids go to bed. If they fall asleep early, it's easy. I also rub her legs nightly. I might do that as we struggle with getting the tornadoes to sleep. Because we are organized and have structure, we'll often throw in a quickie for a midday rendezvous when things interrupt our norm.

If you trusted me with your calendar in Man with Purpose, then you know when you can throw in quickies or schedule one to three-hour sex dates for longer and more intimate connections. Sex weekends are filled with whatever you want. You will have fun, be an incredible lover, be an incredible player, be a super magnet, pull her in, and then build on the fun.

The Toolbox:

Many men today overlook romance, flirting, and banter. Let me help you get started with these tools. Remember, every woman is unique and will appreciate different things differently. Keep the VFC Method in mind and add your own flair. Staying true to who you are is crucial—your most authentic, loving, and masculine self. Be prepared for rejection and continue to provide structure for the marriage you both committed to.

The Embrace/ Kiss:

Men in my program desire more than just sex. Physical intimacy starts with the embrace and the kiss. You should already engage in small touches throughout the day, like in the hall or kitchen. These little moments build up to a meaningful connection. When you're truly on fire again, you'll be excited to see each other after time apart and will take moments to connect throughout the day or night. Make it a goal to kiss your wife at least once a day—a real kiss, separate from sex.

- 10 seconds. I go for 30 seconds - 1 minute.

You can do it when you leave for work or, after you've both brushed your teeth in the morning, when you get home, or before bed. There is no one or right time.

At any random time. Just do it. Ours is very random.

- A Player will stop something he's doing and just give it to her.

- A Player will interrupt her (read the room) and do it.

- A Player will interrupt her conversation or his, do it, and say he just had to.

- A Magnet will not do it at the same time in the same way every day.

- A Lover will connect with his wife and use eye contact at the right moment.

- Start: Grab the back of her neck and pull her in (dominant). Grab the waistline of her pants and pull her in. Grab her cheeks and go for it. You get the point.

- Rejection or Stopping Early: If she rejects it or pulls back, you be the man you are and say: "Hey, get back here". "I'm not done". And get back to it.

- Flat Out Rejection: No big deal. It doesn't affect you. Just be playful and fun, a Player; take Home the Oscar. The kiss will come. You'll get there.

Beyond Flowers:

Flowers are not something to avoid. The problem is that men often use them to apologize, and they become a go-to gift. Here are 30 ideas that go beyond just bringing home flowers. Remember, these are just ideas. Adapt them to fit who you are and your wife's unique preferences. Soon, sending love her way will become second nature. Be both a Lover and a Player. No matter how scared you are, let it go. You are not affected. You have no expectations. Just be you and be awesome.

Written

- Flowers. Don't just pick up roses. Find out what she loves and buy her those. [Hack] Roses have a place, but your wife has a favorite flower. Write a sweet note to go with them.
- Cards. If you take the time to read the card you're picking out and apply it, you'll go a lot further. [Hack] Take extra time to write something meaningful, and you'll be a winner. (YOUR LIST)
- Sticky Notes. Drop one in her purse. On her favorite drink in the fridge. Next to her makeup. You can use one of the things from your Best Friend list. [Hack] When you write something, tell her why.
- Get a dark whiteboard pen and write something on the mirror for her to see from your list. [Hack] Make this into something conversational, and you will have a game going back and forth.
- Get your kids to make something that says, "Daddy loves you." [Hack] She'll love it more if you make one, too.
- Leave a note on her windshield or the driver's side window. [Hack] Take a trip out of your way to leave this in her car when she's at work or the grocery store.
- Send her a love letter in the mail. Actual mail. [Hack] If you do this for a long time, these will make an incredible anniversary gift one day.
- Make a paper airplane and send her a message. [Hack] Don't hit her in the face. Although, the Player might laugh and have fun with it.

- Edit a picture of her and add text to it. [Hack] Make sure she loves the way she looks in it.
- Leave a note (not a letter, not one line, but a message) on the counter for her. [Hack] Pick a different counter than last time.
- Leave her a note (not a letter, not one line, but a message) under her pillow.
- Send one of your kids to her with a note. [Hack] This one is great when she's having a tough day with the kids.

Make Things for Her

- Make her an origami flower.
- Make her favorite animal in origami.
- Make her towel swan on your bed.
- Make her towel hearts on your bed.
- Make her a Modern-Day Mixtape. [Hack] When making a "love song list (for date nights), call that one "Your Names Love List".
- Draw her a picture and leave it on the fridge. [Hack] It's the message that the picture says that counts.
- Make her the card.
- Make her favorite dinner.
- Make her a drink.
- Build something out of wood or metal.

Do Things for Her

- Use Text Message Templates.
- Send her a song when you hear it and think of her. [Hack] Even if you can apply one line in that song, you can send it and share the line that made you think of her.

- Bring her, her favorite treat.
- Leave her a stuffy under her pillow.
- Draw her a bath with rose petals.
- Bring home her favorite dinner.
- Bring home her favorite dinner and make it.
- Do things that your wife loves and get creative. For example, my wife loves cupcakes. So, I will bring her a cupcake with a message for her.
- Use the Date Idea Formula and Mini-Dates especially. [Hack] Apply to you and your best friend.
- Leave a dress (in a box) on the bed with a note: Friday night, 8 pm SHARP. [Hack] Check her closet for her size.
- When she's putting on her underwear, stop her; "Put these on instead" (insert crooked smile) [Hack] Leave them hanging out of the drawer every day until she gets it.
- You run the errand on the way home from work but pick up something along the way.

Text Message Templates

Here are some ideas to keep the Lover and the Player Moving:

- The Lover will make her feel valued, loved, respected... SEEN and HEARD.
- The Player will remind her that she is a sexy woman and, ultimately, you both have needs!
- The Magnet may not always send a message and may not respond immediately; In other words, he's not always available immediately. This is because you're a valuable Man with Purpose, not because you're playing games with alpha or toxic masculinity.

By nature, most men want to communicate less than their wives… so these go a long way. Add your flare, her name, emojis, etcetera, and remember you're not confined to this list. The more you do this, it becomes so freakin' simple.

[Hack] Taking a minute out of your day to call your wife and tell her these things is a game changer. Let it go where it goes. No expectations!

[Hack] Use voice or video so she can hear your tone!

I CANNOT STRESS THIS ENOUGH.

Texting The Next Day:

[BONUS Hack] You can use this at home, at a party, at a restaurant, etc. You have to say them to her face or shout them across the room. Be a Player and watch how this happens.

All you need to do is let your wife know that she was awesome in some way. The point is to follow through with whatever was great, so she knows you are still thinking about her and the great time you had. Using Lords and Morrow Momentum, we address how to do this after a bad night, but this will get you started for the romance side of things. You want to remind her that she is beautiful, fun, intelligent, funny, sexy, etc.

AND DELIVER THEM LIKE YOU ARE FUN, WITTY, SEXY AND PLAYFUL!!!!

- I had so much fun with you last night.
- I really had a great time with you during our date.
- I can't wait to____________again.
- I loved ____________with you yesterday.
- I would like to____________again soon!
- You looked so cute when you ________________.
- You looked gorgeous in your ________________ yesterday.

- Just thought about when we laughed at________________ yesterday. I laughed again.
- You really felt like MY WIFE when you_________________.
- I liked it when you____________ yesterday.
- That meant a lot to me that you______________.
- I really appreciated that you ___________________.
- You worked so hard at ___________________.
- You looked so hot on our date last night.
- I loved hearing you tell me about____________________.
- I liked it when you touched my_________________last night.
- You made me feel like YOUR man when you____________________.
- Your body looked so sexy in your_________________.
- Man, you were HOT last night when you ___________.
- You were a SEXY ASS WOMAN last night.

When texting the same day, just replace words that don't work. So, if it was this morning, replace "yesterday" with "this morning."

Checking In:

- Checking in is an excellent way to maintain a connection with your wife. Don't overcomplicate it. You're just connecting. Let it go where it goes. No expectations!
- Hey Honey, how's your day going?
- What are you up to, Baby?
- I was just thinking of you, my love.
- Miss you today.
- I can't wait to see you.
- Just wanted to say hi.

- You're hot.
- Sexy.
- Thinkin' about you movin'.
- (Pic of you lookin' good) Your man. (Lay off the 'private' pics unless you know for sure it's a go. Most often, it's not worth it).

Texting For Future:

Here again, you are letting your wife know how awesome she is. The difference is you are telling her that you can't wait to see her, showing her that she is your top priority and always on your mind. This is a two-step process. First, express your anticipation. Second, take her response and make her feel empowered—sexy, beautiful, intelligent, funny, confident. Directly tell her what to think in your response to set the tone for what's to come. This gets easier with practice and understanding what your wife struggles with and what she thrives on.

For example, Kathryn struggles with choosing outfits that look the sexiest for me but thrives on feeling intelligent and beautiful. So, I give her a sexy and beautiful combo and then throw in some intelligence. Just remember to direct your wife and set the tone... you are a Player!

- I can't wait to______________tonight. >>> Oh, your butt looks so HOT in that.
- Alright! Date night tonight. I love you, Babe. >>> You're going to have so much fun.
- I'm excited for___________________. >>> I can't wait to see your beautiful smile.
- What are you going to wear for_________________tonight? >>> You look amazing in that.
- You excited for_____________? >>> You deserve it after your day. You work so hard.

- Are you gonna make me laugh as much tonight when we_______________? >>> You were hilarious last time.
- I'm looking forward to___________. >>> I love watching you_________________.
- _________________is going to be great with you. >>> You're always so fun when we _______________.
- You're gonna get it later.
- I'll be home at 8. Bedroom 8:05.
- I need my wife tonight.

Put your style on these messages.

BONUS: Game-Changing Gift Giving:

Never give a pathetic gift again. Men have asked me to share my strategy for my entire adult life. They've asked me to write a book, but it's so easy that there isn't enough to publish, so I'll throw it here!

Generally, men tend to stick to what society has told us women love: jewelry, Coach purses, and expensive stuff or knockoffs. The easy choices. But I have an easier way, and it's much more impressive when it comes to her opening up that gift from you. Here's a little secret, and it might sound crazy... that old saying, "It's the thought that counts"? It's freakin' real.

Now, I'm not saying you can't buy those expensive things or maybe a cheaper version. These are great, and I get them for my wife, too. What I'm saying is that by following this system, you will show her that you listen to her, value her, and love her. It works EVERY time for birthdays, Christmas, Mother's Day, and Valentine's, or you can easily do it more often if you like. If you have the money or if your wife, like Kathryn, has gift-receiving as one of her love languages.

Step by Step:

Keep a Note on Your Phone: I call mine "Kathryn" (she knows not to look at it).

Write Down Everything: Whenever she says she likes something, wants something, or comments on her friend's item, write it down. It doesn't matter if it's a bathing suit she saw on Beach Romance Reality or something small like a type of candy. These small things go great in a stocking or with a card!

[Hack] Google It: Get an image or a link while it's fresh. You now have an ongoing list of ideas your wife will love or at least like, and she will be amazed that you remembered things she mentioned months ago. When you want to really impress her, you can mix and match her loves or passions with these ideas.

Example: This is my favorite story using this system. Kathryn's best gift ever received from me was something she told me she wanted so badly to give her children one day. In the first year of our marriage, she told me her favorite story growing up was The Velveteen Rabbit, and when she had girls, she wanted to give them that book. Fast forward a few years later, when Briar and Vale had their first Christmas with Mama. Yup, they all got a Velveteen Rabbit stuffy and the storybook. I don't think I spent $100, and Kathryn cried for a week and told everyone she knew forever. She couldn't believe that I remembered.

By following this simple strategy, you'll always be prepared with thoughtful, meaningful gifts that show your wife how much you care.

The Level Up:

Now, the level up: Adding things she loves to your list. For this, you need to know your wife. Kathryn LOVES antiques and is passionate about learning. She has five degrees, her Masters, and countless certifications. So, I found encyclopedias from 1914, and she went wild. Again, less than $100.

Neither of these gifts cost a lot of money, and maybe they don't seem crazy exciting to you, but for my wife, I knocked it out of the park, and you better believe it made an impact. The more you know her, the better you get at this. Just take the time to write it down when you have an idea.

[Hack] If it's too expensive, save up for it. It will make it that much more exciting when you “remembered" a year or two later.

Moves to Make Anywhere:

Some of you are lost on what to do around the house or out and about. Start with this list and build on it! Be creative! Always be authentic and true to who you are, but do not be afraid to step outside your comfort zone.

When you get home, pick her up and twirl her. Kiss her. Hold her. Tell her that you missed her. Ask her how her day was. Listen to her.

Draw her a bath: Depending on the privacy she needs, you can rub her in the tub or even sit quietly next to her. Just the simple act of running it for her is amazing, and you are giving her "permission" to relax.

Watching a show: Rub her legs or draw on her back. You'd be surprised at how far it goes if you just draw on her arm. This requires you to sit next to her on the couch!

Morning routine:

Roll over and hold her, kiss her, but don’t press your hard-on into her until you guys have your intimacy figured out!

Know her love language: Deliver the "I love you" in her way of receiving it.

Call or text:

In the middle of the day (or run upstairs if you work from home) and tell her something sweet (see Text Message Templates in the toolbox). Connect with her.

Send a sexy message: Call or text her in the middle of the day (or run upstairs if you work from home) and tell her something sexy (see Text Message Templates in the toolbox). Connect with her.

Press pause:

During the middle of your show and talk to her. Better yet, ask her a question: "How was that conversation with Becky?" or, "I missed it when you were texting about that video you saw on FB. Can you please explain it to me?" or, "You wanted to talk about the kids…"

Surprise date:

Instead of watching a show, pull out one of the Dating Hacks from the toolbox and surprise her with a date.

Dance:

Turn on "your song" when she thinks you're about to turn on a show and dance.

[Hack] I don't particularly like reality TV, but I discovered something exciting when watching these shows with my wife. They spark more conversation, and we laugh a lot more, leading to more adventures.

Unexpected:

"Damn, woman, you need a massage." Then give her one.

[Hack] I use a German accent and tell her, "Z masseuse haz arrived. Yaaaaa. You gonna get z rub down now."

Pull over on the side of the road: Dance with her. As you build your Lover's List, you will continue to learn and know your wife again. This will be who she was, who she's lost along the way, and who she's become.

4 Big Ideas:

Occasionally, it's really fun to go crazy. When you're ready to kick it into high gear, you can do the go-tos: organize a sitter, book the reservations, and surprise her with dinner. Or a trip. Or a dance class she talked about. Now, I love all of those things. If you want to go crazy and be the kind of sweet that levels you up to "to her knees" lust, you've got to think like a romance god. Here are some things I have done that I will share with you. Try them and let me know how incredible they worked for your wife!

These ideas will not, however, go over well if your wife is not attracted to you or still not “in love” again. They also will mean nothing if you haven't at least practiced the lessons you've learned already. Likewise, if she's still so far gone, then she won't even care yet (see my story on the sticky notes).

Book of Messages:

I strongly recommend you start this now with every great text string you have. (Your New Beginning). The backstory: When we first met, we decided we were not going to date. Kathryn wanted a Christian man and children. I wasn't going to go to church, and I had had a vasectomy about 8 or 9 months before meeting her.

She was a member of the gym, so I enjoyed training her, but that was it. A few months later, we began to text. Within 24 hours, we were communicating on text, WhatsApp, and FB messenger. After 2 weeks of round-the-clock messages, I suggested trying a date. We married 1 month later on February 13 for two days of love, back-to-back.

I gave Kathryn a book with all our 6 weeks of messages leading up to our wedding for an anniversary present. We still read that book from time to time. It is the most incredible way to relive your spark from the beginning and IGNITE the passion. If it's been too long, and you could never get those screenshots, just start one today with your new beginning. Remember, it's the thought that counts.

1000 Sticky Notes:

I don't actually know the number when I did this, but remember that big list about your wife I had you make earlier? By now, you've been using it for cards, text messages, etc. This one got tears from some of the wives of men I worked with this past year and some of my friends. Leveled them up big time. For me, not so much, but again, Kathryn didn't believe much of the romance I tried during some of the times in our marriage. Duh.

Get your hands on a few of those sticky notepads. Then, one by one, write on each note. You guessed it; each note has one of the things you wrote down on your lover's list. It's a little tricky, and you can't go right to the end of the notepad because you need to leave them attached until the big day. If you've done your list right, it takes quite a while to transfer all of these over.

When it's time to deliver, stick them all over the house. From the moment she walks in and in every room, everywhere in the house. She will grab them one by one and read them. This is why it was excellent to go random with whatever you thought of. Boom.

Write a Poem or a Song:

Well, I try so hard at this, but well... I'm no rockstar. I've done this a few times, and the point is, she loves it. It's the effort. I actually like to make this more of a fun thing to do. These days, you can Google this, and there are plenty of choices, and AI has changed this dramatically.

Make a Plaque:

When my wife and I started dating, we were really into Dane Cook. We laughed and laughed. We also loved playing music and talked about running away together. So, a few years ago, I made her a plaque. It was so simple. I think $20 delivered. I picked her favorite colors and made it up on Canva.com (which works great for a lot of your toolbox).

It said: "Still Runnin' on our Rockin' Tour, featuring Dane Cook, laughing our asses off. I love you, Baby Cakes." Or something like that. I don't remember. But I remember how she loved reliving our early dates. She didn't cry or anything, but she knew I thought about her so much; I still thought about the beginning. We watched some Dane Cook that night; the rest was wild.

Your Turn:

Now, except for the plaque, these took a lot of effort, and there is no need to go that far. I just wanted to get your head in the game with where this can really go. To really get good at this stuff, you're going to read your wife and share your version of these Hacks. For extra help, join the community, and let's do this together! The point of sharing these, is to show you when you go the extra mile for your wife, she will want to go the extra mile for you and, more importantly, with you.

GO GET YOUR WIFE.

By now, you should be very clear on a few things:

- You are responsible for you. You may not be the problem, but if you are not the solution, you actually are the problem.

- You will never have a wife, yours or another if you don't master yourself first. Go get your wife, but really, go get your life.

- This is a relationship book. You should apply the step-by-step lessons outlined in this book to build every relationship. Just don't sleep with anyone besides your wife. This begins with your relationship with yourself and then everyone else you allow into your life.

- Beyond relationships, you, as a man, need to be an adult. You should make good money, be healthy, and respond in a way you are proud of. Be the man, husband, father, and leader in life you were born to be.

- When you embody the man, you were born to be, I can only describe it as liberating. It truly is freedom. When you've ditched #couplegoals and are #DusruptingDivorce because you've stopped victimizing yourself. In your freedom, you rise up. Get comfortable on the journey. You will never be the man who "gets there;" instead, you'll always continue to Rise.

- Now go. It is your obligation to take what you have learned and lead adult boys out there in the world. I'm charging you with this responsibility because you have been fortunate enough to find me and the work Lords and I are doing. It's no man's fault when he doesn't know or understand. Make every man you come into contact with at least have an opportunity to learn.

- You are obligated to use #MorrowMomentum and make an impact.

- Please feel free to connect with me. Perhaps we'll partner for your impact!

"Thank you for trusting me with your marriage, your life and allowing me to lead you. Now, let's go change the world."

#DisruptingDivorce

Book Links to Free Resources

CassMorrow.com
DisruptingDivorce.com

Https://MorrowMarriage.com/Tools

GO GET YOUR LIFE

USE THIS MOMENTUM &

GO GET YOUR WIFE

Resources

There were far too many resources to include in this book. In the Reset, I suggest dozens of books, courses, coaches, mentors, and influencers. I would like to express my gratitude to each and every one of you. By the time you read this book, I will have sent a private email or direct message from a social media platform.

Disclaimer

I am not associated or affiliated with any of the resources listed below or In the Reset. My interpretations, specifically my adaptations of their wealth of knowledge, are my interpretations alone.

Below are only the resources listed throughout Disrupting Divorce:

Jocko Willink, Extreme Ownership

Travis Neville, Reviving Masculinity

Travis Neville, Mastering Masculinity

Dr. Robert Glover, No More Mr Nice Guy

G.S. Youngblood, The Masculine In Relationship

Destin Gerek, The Evolved Masculine

David Deida, The Way of the Superior Man

D.O.S, The Dead Bedroom Fix

John & Julie Gottman, The Gottman Institute

Emily Nagoski, Come as You Are.

Michelle Kenny, Peace and Parenting, @peaceandparenting

Alex Hormozi, 100M Offer, 100M leads

Cole Dasilva, @coleluisdasilva

Brian Mark, @therealbrianmark

Jeremy Minor, 7th Level

Andy Elliot, The Elliot Group

Dave Ramsey, Ramsey Solutions

Gary Chapman: The Five Love Languages

Did you find value in Disrupting Divorce? Please help Kathryn, Lords and me with your valuable 5-Star Review.

Your review may cause the ripple effect needed to truly reach our goal: Disrupting Divorce.

God Bless,

Cass.

Made in the USA
Columbia, SC
25 October 2024